TRUST

THE

PLAN

Jeremiah 17:7-8
Titus 2:11-15

Becoming a Holy Habitation

& More Than a Conqueror

J. D. HINSON

TRUST THE PLAN: Becoming a Holy Habitation & More Than a Conqueror

Copyright © 2019 by J. D. Hinson

All rights reserved. This book is protected by the copyright laws of the United States of America. No Portion of this book may be stored electronically, transmitted, copied, reproduced or reprinted for commercial gain or profit. Only the use of short quotations or occasional page copying for personal or group study is allowed without permission.

Unless otherwise noted, all Scripture quotations are from The Holy Bible, New King James Version. Copyright © 1982 by Thomas Nelson, Inc. Used by permission. All rights reserved.

Cover design by Luke Gajary

Cover picture: Shutterstock Enhanced License.
Inside image by unknown author: Fair Use licensed CC-BY-SA

Contact Information
lookingup@reagan.com
facebook.com/J.D. Hinson

ISBN: 978-1-7331349-0-3 (paperback)
ISBN: 978-1-7331349-1-0 (eBook)

Library of Congress Control Number: 2019916776

Printed in the United States of America

Dedication

To my beautiful wife, Jan,
our children, grandchildren, and
our son, Talmadge, who lives with Jesus.
All of you are the true treasures of heaven.

Acknowledgments

The writing of this book is not only the thoughts and experiences of the author. There is always a strong support group, and I have been blessed with such a group, Marcia Kendall, founder of Flame Fellowship International and Pastor Chuck Farina of New Hope Church. I am eternally grateful for their work of proof reading, insightful comments and suggestions. I also want to thank Smadar Yoel Cohen for her help on the Hebrew letter portion. The Lord bless you all for your encouragement.

My amazing wife, Jan, spent countless hours formatting and editing. Without her help it may never have come to print. This book is part of our story. Thank you for believing in me and being a constant strength in every part of this journey. I love you dearly.

Contents

Foreword by Pastor Chuck Farina..........................vi
Chapter 1 – The Encounter......................................1

Part One – Understanding the Plan

Chapter 2 – The Journey Begins...............................7
Chapter 3 – Purpose of Creation.............................17
Chapter 4 – God's Mandate......................................31
Chapter 5 – Lost Inheritance..................................47
Chapter 6 – Deliverance from Bondage....................61

Part Two – Engaging the Plan

Chapter 7 – Cleansing the Temple...........................81
Chapter 8 – Cursing the Fig Tree.............................97
Chapter 9 – Facing the Mountain............................119

Part Three – Trusting the Plan

Chapter 10 – Our Family's Journey..........................137
Chapter 11 – Taking Your Inheritance......................183
Chapter 12 – Living in Your Inheritance................... 193

Additional Testimonies

Hannah's Testimony..201
Travis' Testimony...209
Jan's Testimony..221
Prayer, Blessings and Declarations..........................229
End Notes...233

Foreword

Every believer is going to go through events, circumstances, and even seasons in their lives when God doesn't make sense. And even though we know "intellectually" that God is in control, that He has good plans for our future, and that He is for us…every emotion is screaming to the contrary. This book is a rally call for every person who has ever questioned God's plan for their life. I'm pretty sure that is all of us.

In his book, *Trust the Plan*, J.D. takes us on a journey, inviting us behind the scenes of some of the darkest hours of his family's life. It is a candid look at how they encountered God and His all sufficient grace through very difficult circumstances. He reveals how it was in those dark seasons that he learned to trust the Lord and His plan even when it didn't make sense.

I have had the privilege of being a pastor to J.D. and Jan Hinson over the past several years. As I have observed their lives and ministry, J.D. and Jan have modeled so much humility, wisdom and genuine anointing. I have seen a level of maturity and security in Christ in their lives that is so uncommon. It was in reading this book that I came to understand **how** Christ formed His character in them.

J.D. presents profound revelation on the overarching eternal plan of God and brings it into everyday application that will give you a reason to lean again into the arms of our loving Father. There is a *plan*, and as we once again learn to trust the Lord, we will see God's plan unfold in our lives as Jeremiah promised.

Jeremiah 29:11 NLT - For I know the plans I have for you," says the LORD. "They are plans for good and not for disaster, to give you a future and a hope.

God is calling His body to rise to the challenge of His original mandate. It is time we rise up and take the dominion God gave and Jesus restored. I believe that will only happen as we realize what was lost, how God got it back, and how we can live from that inheritance each day. J.D. does an amazing job through this book of showing us that path.

Get ready to change. You can't read this book and not change. Truth affects us. Jesus said, "...you will know the truth, and the truth will set you free." Revealed truth will set you free to trust. Truth will give you direction to recapture your destiny. Truth will show you the path and give you the courage to walk it out!

I pray you will move past the wounds, scars and fears of the past and "Trust the Plan." As you do, you will become more than a conqueror in Christ Jesus!

Chuck Farina

Pastor New Hope Church

Abilene, Texas

Chapter One

The Encounter

Words. *It was just words.* How can three little words have such an impact? It was November 12, 1998, and I was working in Dallas, Texas at the district office of the organization of which I am a part when I received a phone call from my wife, Jan. What she said still rings in my ears as clear as it did then. She said, "Talmadge had an accident." Thinking of his little yellow car which he had purchased six weeks before I asked, "How bad was it?" She said, "Talmadge is dead."

Talmadge Paul, our youngest son, was only three months away from his seventeenth birthday. My heart stopped for a moment, and my mind went blank. What happens to you physically and emotionally upon hearing these words is something I never desire to live through again. Words are totally inadequate to describe the darkness we found ourselves living. Never could we have imagined this would become part of our family's history. Now what? We were facing a darkness that demanded an answer, and we had a choice to make.

Many people have experienced the suddenness of devastating news, so we are not alone in this type of life-changing event. These things happen in our broken and fallen world. However, I must emphasize this. God **did not** cause the accident. Could He have prevented it? Yes, He could have prevented it. But questions of this nature become snares and must be avoided for they will lead you into a maze of bitterness. **Never allow the darkness to define who God is.** Never forget that the Father's unwavering love and care is an unshakable truth. This should assure us that even in our darkest hour He is with us.

Two months after Talmadge's accident in January of 1999, our church was involved in a service with four area churches in Wichita Falls, Texas. I was physically there but not mentally. During the praise and worship, as everyone was standing except me, the Lord gently asked me, "Will you trust Me?" I did not know what to say. I thought I was trusting. I had faith and believed life would get better over time. Is not faith and trust the same thing? Little did I realize the significance of His question. The Father was watering His Word (seed) which had been planted in my spirit many years earlier and was leading me to a deeper understanding of trust. He knew many days ahead would be stormy, yet there would also be days of sunshine. He is true to His word, *"I will never leave you, nor forsake you."* He sees the deep hidden areas of our heart, and what He saw in me that day was a little boy trembling with fear and uncertainty under the crushing weight of sorrow. My faith was under assault. Even with all of the assurances He had given, questions still remained. What happens now? How do we live? Psalm 56:3, *"When I am afraid, I will trust in You."* But HOW do you do that? As I sat silently on the pew while everyone else around me in the service was singing, I felt His presence. He said nothing else beyond, "Will you trust Me?" He was silent, waiting for my response. In my mind it seemed He started walking, then stopped, turned and looked at me as if to say, "Well, what are you going to do?" What could I do? My emotions were raw. I chose to walk after Him. Where was He going? I did not know, but it had to be better than the place I was in.

This part of my family's story is not just about me. My wife and two grown children were each navigating this darkness as well, and I had to be willing to trust Him with their care for at that moment I was not capable. I chose to follow the Lord into the unknown and held to this one truth. He loves me even in this darkness of emotions, and God's indescribable mercy and grace held me.

The Lord was inviting me to move off the river bank into a deep, continuous flowing river of trust. His invitation was unsettling to my natural mind. If ever I was going to trust Him, it needed to be now. I was reminded that He knew me before I was conceived and called me by name. Little did I know at the time, but I had begun a journey of discovery that would take twenty years to the month to fully comprehend. He does have a plan.

Sixteen years after this encounter in 1999, on Palm Sunday of 2015, I was reading Matthew 21:12-22. I had been a pastor for many years and was familiar with the passage I was reading. These verses describe the events on the first two days of the last week of Jesus' life before His crucifixion, death, burial and resurrection. As I was reading about the cursing of the fig tree in verse 19, the Holy Spirit stopped me and asked, "Do you know why Jesus cursed the fig tree?" The question took me off guard as I was not prepared for it. The Holy Spirit knew this and proceeded to give me insight. This began a journey through the scriptures I thought I knew, only to discover I had just been wading in the river with the water barely lapping over my ankles. As the Holy Spirit opened up my understanding to this portion of scripture, I have been amazed at the deep and rich wonders of the Lord's plan.

As the years have gone by, I have come to realize more fully that my family's story is not any different than yours or anyone else who has gone on before. How our family has navigated life has not been perfect by any means. We have had victories, disappointments and open rebellion, but the plans and purposes of God have been a rod of protection and a staff of comfort. In fact, our story and yours mirror those in scripture. We live in the twenty-first century, and their story seems like ancient history, but the unseen powers are the same. The conflicts we face are no different than theirs, and the weapons and tactics the evil one uses against us are the same as with them.

There is much more to my family's story. How we lived before the accident and through other difficult circumstances afterwards is revealed in later chapters. How our lives have been shaped and molded is part of the Matthew 21:12-22 narrative, and to have a clear understanding of this passage we must begin at the beginning.

Understanding

the

Plan

Chapter Two

The Journey Begins

In the beginning God, a phrase we all know well. We can rest assured that "in the beginning" God had a plan which included His creation of mankind. We are not as familiar with the events in the Garden of Eden as we should be. You may think that God's plan was derailed, and He had to go to "Plan B." Know this, dear friend. God does not have a "Plan B." <u>God has a plan</u>. From Genesis to Revelation we see God's original plan and purpose displayed. His story (history) of love and redemption is woven throughout every book of the Bible as He instructs mankind on how to live. These are divine patterns of the will of God repeated over and over throughout scripture. The faces and places may change, but God's original plan and purpose has not changed, and nothing can stop its fulfilment. We may not fully understand it, but you and I, here and now, are very much a part of the divine purpose that was birthed in eternity past.

What we see as setbacks, God uses as an opportunity to display His almighty power through His marvelous grace, mercy, compassion and love. He is leading us to the day when

He will display His handiwork in us to all creation. Until that day arrives, we are invited to participate in the very life and heart of His plan. This book will take you on a journey. You will discover that YOU are included in His plan, as the days of your life were written in God's book before any one of them came to be. Psalms 139:16.

A study of Matthew 21:12-22 will be our primary focus for it was out of that Palm Sunday encounter in 2015 that this manuscript was birthed. I do not say my understanding of this portion of scripture is complete. It is not. The subject was birthed in eternity past and runs through to eternity future, and it will be a continual revelation to those who seek it.

This passage describes three events that took place on the first two days of the last week of Jesus' life on Earth. On those first two days of that last week, Jesus did three things. He cleansed the Temple, cursed the fig tree, and gave specific instructions on how to remove the mountain. Our main questions will be why did Jesus do these things, and what was He trying to convey to His disciples?

In order for us to understand Matthew 21:12-22 we need to take a journey back to the events in the Garden of Eden, as well as the Exodus from Egypt, and the wilderness wondering of the Jewish people. The purpose in looking at these are essential to our understanding. These Old Testament historical events are like mirrors into our own lives and are imperative to our understanding of God's intended purpose for us. Each of us are on a journey to our own personal destiny with a destination and an inheritance. We have a part to play in this life, and it is not just a flash in the pan. God has a plan for you and me here on this Earth, and His purpose is for us to become a new creation like one never known or imagined before. My intention is to get us off the bench and into the fight of pulling down strongholds, taking back what was stolen from us, and living a life where we become "more than conquerors" in Christ Jesus.

The cleansing of the Temple, the cursing of the fig tree, and the mountain encounter during this last week before the crucifixion were not just a response to the sin of mankind. It was God's judgment directed at the evil one and his open rebellion. The rebellion that flowed out of the heart of the adversary, Satan, is still being displayed and lived out in the lives of his offspring. The adversary was then and is still declaring his rebellion against God. Isaiah describes his rebellion in this way.

Isaiah 14:13
"For you have said in your heart:
'I will ascend into heaven,
I will exalt my throne above the stars of God;
I will also sit on the mount of the congregation on the farthest sides of the north'."

The warring of two spiritual seeds and two kingdoms has not abated but has increased in fury, and mankind, the crown of creation, is the battleground. This special creation and its purpose are eternal. No one is exempt from the conflict. Whether you realize it or not you are involved, and furthermore, you are the prize.

God had His plan of redemption and restoration in place long before anything was created. God does not react to anything. He responds, and His response will always be for life and light and for His glory. God's purpose for humanity is for us to live the abundant life He intended here on Earth not just when we get to heaven.

In this study you will discover that the place where the original rebellion occurred is still with us today. The conflict is real, and Satan's purpose is still the same. But remember, none of this took God by surprise. So, take courage; you are not alone in your journey through this life. God has a plan for you, and He desires to reveal it. John 1:4 says, *"In Him was life, and the life was the light of men."*

Understanding why Jesus cleansed the Temple and cursed the fig tree is crucial to our warfare. We need not be ignorant of Satan's devises. We serve a risen Savior who openly put to shame the forces of evil.

An Invitation Is Given

Before we can delve into Matthew 21, we must first understand the players and exactly what happened "in the beginning." Charles (Chuck) Missler, Ph.D. wrote of the unity, placement, and importance of the Holy Scriptures in his book, *I, Jesus, an Autobiography,* on page 114, Koinonia House Institute.

> *"It is 66 separate books penned by some 40 authors spanning several thousand years. Yet in these 66 books every number, every place name, every detail, every Hebrew letter or fraction of a letter is part of a tightly engineered design, tailored for our learning, our discovery and our amazement of the actual author of this work."*

Dr. Missler also states on page 117 of his book, *I, Jesus, an Autobiography.*

> *"The Jewish rabbis say that they will not really understand the Scriptures until the Messiah comes. But when he comes, he will not only interpret each passage for us, he will interpret the very words; he will even interpret the very letters themselves; in fact, he will interpret the spaces between the very letters themselves!"*

When we study or read the scriptures, we may find ourselves passing over some "minor" detail only later to find the "minor" detail held the key to a deeper understanding of the passage. It is also possible to believe we have exhausted a portion of scripture and have a complete understanding with nothing more to be learned. Have you ever been so familiar with a passage that you read right over it? I think we all have.

Of course, we must be careful <u>not</u> to read into a text something that is not there, but we do not need to be afraid to ask the Holy Spirit to teach us as we prayerfully study and examine scripture. One lesson I learned in Bible college was the Bible will interpret itself. This is not to say we should not use outside resources, but our first place of reference is the scriptures themselves. The scriptures tell us God and His ways are past finding out.

> *Romans 11:33*
> *"O, the depth of the riches both of the wisdom and knowledge of God! How unsearchable are his judgments and His ways past finding out!"*

> *Proverbs 25:2*
> *"It is the glory of God to conceal a matter but the glory of kings is to search out a matter."*

Study of the Holy Scriptures is a lifetime journey. How marvelous it is to daily discover the glory within each verse and to realize each word within the text is an adventure into the depths of the knowledge of God. I am so grateful for the research of past and present theologians. They give us added insight and have placed markers and helps for deeper understanding. Yet, only one teacher has the full revelation of the scriptures, and He is the Holy Spirit who moved on holy men of God to write and who is the one sent to lead and guide us into all truth.

> *2 Peter 1:21*
> *"For prophecy never came by the will of man, but holy men of God spoke [as they were] moved by the Holy Spirit."*
>
> *John 14:26*
> *"But the Helper, the Holy Spirit, whom the Father will send in My name, He will teach you all things, and bring to your remembrance all things that I said to you."*
>
> *John 16:13*
> *"However, when He, the Spirit of truth, has come, He will guide you into all truth."*

While it is true that we mortals may not know every scripture in the Bible, we all have our favorite verses. Many of them we have put to memory, and we can recall them as needed or as a cliché. God's Word can give us a needed lift when we are down. However, when life's harder issues step in, those same scriptures can seem to become wishful thinking. You do not have to be involved in public ministry to know this. Just being around people and listening to what they say, you realize everyone has life issues. We may differ one from another, but we all have battles and questions just the same. We can live under secret burdens we were never meant to carry all the while trudging along through life seemingly going nowhere. Have you ever felt this way? I certainly have at times. We think, "Is this the abundant life to which Jesus was referring?" Certainly not. Why is it then that I seem to live in endless cycles of battle after battle with nothing ever changing?

First of all, though our Lord never promised us a trouble-free life, <u>He did intend for us to be overcomers</u>. In fact, He said in John 16:33, *"In the world you will have tribulation; but be encouraged, I have overcome the world."* This was spoken before the crucifixion, and these words were not a last-minute pep talk. Jesus was telling them and us, you can and will live differently *in* Me. It will not come on a silver platter. Life is going to be intense at times, but *"Do not fear little flock, for it is your Father's good pleasure to give you the Kingdom."* Luke 12:32.

The discoveries I put forth are not a theory to my family and me. We have lived in the marvelous riches of God's grace through difficult trials. I am not writing this because we have attained breakthroughs in every area of our lives. On the contrary, each of us have had personal victories and setbacks. Life is a wonderful gift from God, and it is to be lived. But living in this world produces many unexpected moments. The question is how do we respond? In this book I have shared our story as candidly as possible, our journey, our victories, our set-backs, and what our Lord has taught us along the way. Our story is not complete as we are still writing it. We are living the adventure. I hope to encourage you and to help you see the death and resurrection of Jesus in a fresh way. But more importantly, I hope you see what He has done for you, and that He has prepared good works for you to walk in. The Lord is inviting each of us to live a life beyond our wildest imagination.

I am reminded of a sermon by Reverend Paris Reidhead titled, "Ten Shekels and a Shirt." In the message he recalls being in prayer after going as a missionary to Africa. He was quite upset with the Lord for sending him where no one was interested in his message. As he recalls, the Lord told him He knew they would not listen and were sinners deserving hell, but He loved them. The Lord did not send him to Africa for their sake but for His sake saying, "Do I not deserve the reward of my suffering?" The reward is the souls of men, but so is our obedience. Paris goes on to say that the message God breathed into his heart changed his whole perspective on ministry.

As the redeemed of God, we should live our lives in the fullness of the cross and the power and depths and riches of His grace. This is what I want. I do not want to just exist. I want to know Jesus in His fullness, live in His presence and experience His victory in all of my life. How about you?

We have an adversary who is holding people in bondage, and he brings death and destruction upon so many. We live in too much defeat, when the way has been opened to live a life of holiness - not a superficial, shallow life but a life abundant in fruitfulness and victory.

The conclusions I put forth have come out of personal study and observation of patterns in scripture. I offer them for you to consider in your own study. You may agree with some thoughts I put forth or none at all. I am not presenting one denominational view above another or of any independent fellowship. But I would encourage you to carefully read and ask the Holy Spirit for fresh anointing and insight into the Word of God. Take all of the research of all the theologians of all time and put it all together, and we have not even begun to understand the eternal depths of God's Word. This study is a journey with an intended destination, and I invite you to join me on this journey of discovery.

With that being said, I am a Pentecostal pastor ordained with the International Church of the Foursquare Gospel. However, I was raised in a Southern Baptist church. My wife and I pastored thirty-two years and now speak in area churches across denominational lines when invited. What I see is people of all church affiliations are hungry for a fresh breath of the Holy Spirit, and many are looking for answers to lifelong struggles. We may not always agree on every point, but what we do agree on is this. This life is not the end of the matter, and we all need help and guidance as we live out God's plan.

One day we will see Jesus in all His glory, and my desire is to hear Him say, "Well done, good and faithful servant. Enter into the joys of the Lord." I believe this is the desire of all who truly know Him as Lord. If this manuscript brings fresh insight or encouragement, I am blessed to be a vessel in the hands of Almighty God and will give Jesus all the glory. Are you ready? Caleb was.

Joshua 14:9-12
"9 And Moses swore on that day, saying, 'Surely the land on which your foot has trodden shall be an inheritance for you and your children forever, because you have wholly followed the Lord my God.
10 And now, behold, the Lord has kept me alive, just as he said, these forty-five years since the time that the Lord spoke this word to Moses, while Israel walked in

the wilderness. And now, behold, I am this day eighty-five years old.

[11] I am still as strong today as I was in the day that Moses sent me; my strength now is as my strength was then, for war and for going and coming.
[12] So now give me this hill country of which the Lord spoke on that day, for you heard on that day how the Anakim were there, with great fortified cities. It may be that the Lord will be with me, and I shall drive them out just as the Lord said."

Chapter Three

Purpose of Creation

Everyone has a favorite story or movie. In fact, we enjoy them over and over. Some have read or watched them so many times they are able to say or quote the story word for word. We find ourselves drawn into each page or scene. We become active participants in the action. We experience all the emotions of being there, and we find ourselves trying to figure out how to overcome the villain. As we become familiar with the plot and actors, there is a subconscious knowing it will all end well. Even as the plot takes many twists and turns and has sudden unexpected moments, we know the final pages or scenes will be pleasant. So, when rereading or reviewing the story many times, it becomes safe. We know the hero of the story is smarter and stronger and has a secret weapon that will bring him the ultimate and complete victory.

Such are the events of the "Easter" season beginning with Palm Sunday and the Triumphant Entry of Jesus into Jerusalem. We have seen all manner of plays and movies describing these events to the best of our understanding.

Some will attend an Easter service who will not attend church at any other time. It is as if they have an Old Testament attitude of offering up a yearly sacrifice similar to what the Israelites did at Passover for sins committed the previous year. This is a testament to the deep longing for hope and assurance they will be admitted into heaven when they die. The familiar story soothes their heart for a moment as they are reminded of what Christ did. But without a full conversion experience, the person is only a spectator watching a movie. They are just observers and not participants in the story. What they fail to realize is THEY are part of the story. Even now, the truth of those days is being lived out in their lives. Both you and I have a part in this story, because it is about us. The truth is Jesus did not die and rise from the dead just to give us fire insurance. There is a much, much larger and divine plan. Father God is calling us to be partakers in a life that is far beyond anything we could imagine.

The Clash of Two Kingdoms

All of the gospel writers have written about the events leading up to Christ's crucifixion, and each one described the details in the way they lived them. The book of Matthew has 28 chapters, and the last 8 chapters (almost a third of the book) are given solely to the last week of the life of Jesus, His death and resurrection, and His final instructions to His followers.

On those first two days of this last week of Jesus' presence amongst them, He set the final stage to empower His disciples and His church to prevail against the gates of hell and pull-down strongholds. God desires an unblemished bride as a dwelling place and a holy habitation for His presence. This ultimate clash of two kingdoms was displayed at creation - the Kingdom of Light and Truth and the kingdom of darkness and lies. All of humanity is in one of these two kingdoms. There is no middle ground. We often hear the phrase, "That person is straddling the fence." Let me be very clear about this. THERE IS NO FENCE. A person cannot be almost saved or live in both places. Jesus said in John 3:3, *"Most assuredly, I say to you, unless one is born again, he cannot see the Kingdom of God."*

When the Holy Spirit begins to convict of sin, that is the appointed day for salvation and repentance. God is gracious and will pursue lost sheep, but it is dangerous to delay leaving the kingdom of darkness or to attempt making "deals" with God. To be careless with one's eternal soul is unwise. The way of escape is offered. Take it.

Choose Wisely

There are many things about ourselves in which we had no choice, for instance our name, date of birth or ethnicity. We did not choose our parents nor the environment in which we lived nor many other factors that began to mold our lives. However, by God's design we were given the ability to choose.

This ability allows us to be shaped by many outside influences through the things we see, hear and imagine. These three influences are gateways to developing who we are and how we respond to life. Our mind set, world view, and morals are all influenced by the things we see and hear or perceive to be true. False imaginations of the mind can develop and control our actions and words.

It is through these gateways of influence that the adversary entered and tempted Eve with the intended purpose to get her to question God's directive. With so many things coming at us, we too will begin to make our own choices, and choices have eternal consequences, not only for us but for those around us. Whether we realize it or not, what we see, hear, and imagine, along with the words we speak will build up or tear down and will bring victory or defeat.

> Luke 6:45
> "⁴⁵ A good man out of the good treasure of his heart brings forth good; and an evil man out of the evil treasure of his heart brings forth evil. For out of the abundance of the heart his mouth speaks."

God Has A Purpose for Me?

People live out, not only <u>what</u> they believe, but <u>who</u> they believe. Our natural minds believe what we are taught or what we perceive to be true. Yet, the greatest truth is the revealed truth of God brought to us by the Holy Spirit who is the Spirit of Truth. John 16:13. Our lives bear the fruit of many sowers, and we pass that same fruit on to future generations. In other words, the source or kingdom you live in and draw your life from has eternal consequences. There is no escaping it. Your words matter. Your choices matter. Your life matters.

It is difficult to understand the full extent of the divine plan and purpose that God had in mind for the creation of humanity. He alone knows how to bring us to completeness, and He wants you and I to discover our individual part in His plan. Our daily relationship with the Lord is not an option if we want to fulfill our own God-given purpose. This is one of the most important factors in our discovery.

Coming to this understanding should cause us to realize that we were not created just to occupy a small segment of time and space. We were created to come into unity with God's Spirit and to become one with the Father. Many people become discontented or bored with life, not realizing God has given us an invitation to live a life so full that not even the cleverest scriptwriter could pen the adventures.

1 Corinthians 2:9
"But as it is written, 'Eye has not seen, nor ear heard, nor have entered into the heart of man the things which God has prepared for those who love Him'."

Extreme Intervention Required

What Jesus did before His death and resurrection in cleansing the Temple and cursing the fig tree are part of God's response to the events in the Garden of Eden. Much has been written about the nature of the sin committed in the garden. It is not my intention to delve into that, except to say, a very grievous and vile action took place there. Pastor Carl Gallups in his book, *The Gods of Ground Zero,* is a tremendous resource for this.

We tend to focus mainly on the temptation and the resulting fall that lead to the spiritual separation of man from God. We need to realize the seed of corruption planted in our world on that fateful day has produced a spiritual blindness in the natural mind which one cannot begin to grasp. The scene painted in our minds may be little more than the plucking and eating of a fruit and is not a big deal. I mean, what was God so upset about anyway? Good question. What was lost in our fellowship with God when man chose to participate with darkness and open rebellion was our connection to LIFE, the very breath of God. Living is only existing without being connected to our Creator, the Giver of Life. Matthew 21:12-22 is about reconnection.

It is imperative we move away from "flannel board" stories and embark on a pursuit to FIND Him and to KNOW Him for HE is our Life. Until that is our passion, there will be the temptation to transform Him into our image and for our purposes. If we do that, then we will have only ashes of what could have been.

> *Romans 8:19-21*
> *"^{19} For the earnest expectation of the creation eagerly waits for the revealing of the sons of God.*
> *^{20} For the creation was subjected to futility, not willingly, but because of Him who subjected it in hope;*
> *^{21} because the creation itself also will be delivered from the bondage of corruption into the glorious liberty of the children of God."*

The only means for full restoration was so extreme it took God Himself coming to Earth in a body of flesh to redeem His creation.

> *John 1:14*
> *"And the Word became flesh and dwelt among us, and we beheld His glory, the glory as of the only begotten of the Father, full of grace and truth."*

Hebrews 10:5-7
"⁵ Sacrifice and offering You did not desire, but a body You have prepared for Me.
⁶ In burnt offerings and sacrifices for sin You had no pleasure.
⁷ Then said I, 'Behold, I have come. In the volume of the book it is written of Me, to do Your will, O God."

Garden of Eden

It all began in Eden at a place known as the Garden of Eden. It is in this place where we meet the principle characters of the Bible. Understanding what happened in the Garden of Eden after creation will give us the perspective, we need to uncover the truths in our Matthew 21 study. God's plan is revealed through every player and action that took place at the fall, and it will have its completion on the Great Day of the Lord.

Scholars have debated about the exact location of the Garden of Eden for many years. We seem to have a pretty good picture of its general location recorded in scripture. However, this is before the flood, and over time the rivers have changed their courses, and landscapes have eroded.

Genesis 2:8
"⁸ The LORD God planted a garden eastward in Eden, and there He put the man whom He had formed.

Genesis 2:10-14
¹⁰ Now a river went out of Eden to water the garden, and from there it parted and became four riverheads.

> *¹¹ The name of the first is Pishon; it is the one which skirts the whole land of Havilah, where there is gold.*
> *¹² And the gold of that land is good. Bdellium and the onyx stone are there.*
> *¹³ The name of the second river is Gihon; it is the one which goes around the whole land of Cush.*
> *¹⁴ The name of the third river is Hiddekel; it is the one which goes toward the east of Assyria. The fourth river is the Euphrates."*

The importance of the garden cannot be over stated. Adam had fellowship with God in Eden. It was there that Adam learned of his divine purpose to live and function as the ruler and guardian of God's physical creation. The Garden of Eden was the central focal point of all administration for this world, and the central focus of the garden was the Mountain of God. Simply stated. Eden is Israel, and the Garden of Eden is Jerusalem.

The reader may have already come to this conclusion, but if not, a thoughtful study of scripture makes it evident. Jerusalem is the most contested piece of real-estate on the planet. Yet, it does not have any natural resources nor is it a major city of trade. Wars have been fought over this ancient location for millennium. Three major religions lay claim to Jerusalem - Judaism, Christianity and Islam. There is not a day goes by that Jerusalem or Israel are not in the news. It is also the only city to which we are instructed to pray for its peace. Psalm 122:6. Whoever controls Jerusalem will rule the world for a short time during the Tribulation. Jerusalem is the city to which Jesus will return and set up His earthly kingdom. This is God's city, and His Holy Mountain, Mount Zion, is there. Furthermore, the Gihon Spring flows out from the city to this day.

We may well understand that there is an unseen spiritual kingdom, but I also believe the unseen is more real than the shadow we live in. In the plan of God, He has chosen to meet with man in our sphere, our physical realm. We must come to understand that what we see in the physical is completely and eternally connected to the spiritual.

Two temple structures have been built and destroyed in Jerusalem. One more is yet to be built which the antichrist, the son of perdition, will sit in and reign from. When this occurs, Satan will think he has finally reached his goal, "the throne of God," but it will be short lived.

I have a good friend, Pastor/Rabbi Bruce Tentzer, who pastors Hope 4 Life Foursquare Church and Tikvah L'Chaim, a Messianic congregation in Abilene, Texas. When I approached him about my thoughts, he said that in some Jewish circles, they believe that Jerusalem is the Garden of Eden, and Israel is Eden. My wife and I have another Jewish friend, Smadar Yoel Cohen, who was born in Afula, Israel and who was in the Israeli Defense Force until she was discharged and came to America. I told her of my thoughts, and she said I was absolutely correct. Not only is Jerusalem the Garden of Eden, but it is also the center of the universe. With this thought in mind I proceeded to search this matter out.

In Dr. Michael Heiser's book, *The Unseen Realm*, on pages 46-47 he writes concerning the mountain of God.

> *"Yahweh could also be found on mountains (Sinai or Zion). In Psalm 48:1-2, Jerusalem, the city of God, is said to be located in the 'heights of the north (Taspon in Hebrew)'*

"Mount Zion is the 'mountain of assembly,' again located in the 'heights of the north' (Isaiah 14:13). At Sinai, Moses and the others saw the seated God of Israel, under whose feet was a pavement 'like sapphire tile work and like the very heavens for clearness' (Exodus 24:9-10).

"The Garden of Eden, of course, is a lush, well-watered habitation (Genesis 2:5-14). Ezekiel 28:13 mentions the garden of Eden ('garden of god'), but then adds the description that the garden of God is 'God's holy mountain' Ezekiel 28:14. We naturally think of God's mountain as Mount Sinai or Mount Zion. When it comes to garden imagery, the latter is spoken of in Edenic terms. Like Eden, Mount Zion is also described as a watery habitation. (Isaiah 33:20-22; Ezekiel 47:1-12; Zechariah 14:8; Joel 3:18). Whether Sinai or Zion, the mountain of God is in effect his temple."

The Uniqueness of Man

At creation mankind was the original temple of God's presence on Earth. We were created in His image and likeness for a divine reason. As imagers of His reflection we were to establish God's presence on the Earth and were impowered to live extraordinary lives of victory and authority over creation.

However, we lost that position at the fall. It is God's intention to bring full restoration and deliverance back to those who choose Him. In order to do this the Lord God must first cleanse His Temple (us). It is at salvation we become the Temple of God once again. God desires a holy habitation housing His presence with authority to rule and reign with Him. The apostle Paul makes it clear that our body becomes the temple of God at salvation.

> *1 Corinthians 6:19-20*
> *"¹⁹ Or do you not know that your body is the temple of the Holy Spirit who is in you, whom you have from God, and you are not your own?*
> *²⁰ For you were bought at a price; therefore, glorify God in your body and in your spirit, which are God's."*

I am not minimizing the importance of a physical temple on Earth. It has great prophetic significance. As beautiful as temples and churches are, these earthly structures were not meant to be the focus for eternity. Man, however, created in the image of God will continue forever. See Genesis 1:27.

The creation of man was unique. Psalm 139:14 says we are fearfully and wonderfully made. We were created to interact with God on a level of intimacy completely different. No other part of creation was created to image God, and the angels find this mysterious.

> *1 Peter 1:12*
> *"It was revealed to them that they were serving not themselves but you, in the things that have now been announced to you through those who preached the good news to you by the Holy Spirit sent from heaven, things into which angels long to look."*

Let us take a look at how different we are from the rest of creation. When God created man, He formed him out of clay.

Strong's Concordance #H 3335. In Genesis 2:7 the word "formed" means to squeeze into shape or to mold into a form as a potter.

Then the Lord *"breathed"* into this clay form, and man became a living soul. Breathe in the Hebrew is "naw-fakh' and means:

Strong's Concordance #5301, naw-fakh - to puff, to inflate, to blow hard or blow, to breathe.

In the Septuagint (the Greek translation of the Hebrew Bible) "breathed" carries the same meaning. Our Creator literally formed the crown of His creation with His hands and breathed His breath into him. The angels had witnessed God speak creation into existence, but with man God breathed His breath into him. You have to wonder what the angelic hosts of heaven must have thought about Adam, especially when it became apparent, he was given a world to rule over. The angels were not given such authority over a kingdom. Did this further infuriate the anointed cherub who rebelled against God? Adam and Eve had the very breath of God in them which literally clothed them in the brilliant light of God's Spirit.

After the resurrection Jesus **breathed** on His disciples and said, "Receive the Holy Spirit" imparting back into them the presence and light of God's Spirit, thus preparing them to be filled with the fire of the Holy Spirit which had been promised. Luke 3:16. The Greek word John used for "breathed" in John 20:22 is the same word used in the Greek Septuagint for "breathed" in Genesis 2:7. Arthur Pink describes "breathed" in John 20:22 like this.

Exposition of the Gospel of John by Arthur W. Pink, page 1100.

> *"The Greek word here used is employed nowhere else in the New Testament, but is the very one used by the Septuagint translators of Genesis 2:7.*
>
>> *'And the Lord God formed man of the dust of the ground, and breathed into his nostrils the breath of life; and man became a living soul.'*
>
> *There, man's original creation was completed by this act of God. Who, then, can fail to see that here in John 20, on the day of the Savior's resurrection, the new creation had begun, begun by the Head of the new creation, the last Adam acting as 'a quickening spirit' (1 Cor. 15:45)?"*

Then, on the Day of Pentecost, the Holy Spirit was poured out without measure and set a holy fire upon each one gathered in the upper room. Acts 2:4. This brought about the fulfillment of Joel 2:28-29 which continues to this day.

In Dr. Michael Heiser's book, *The Unseen Realm*, on pages #40-43 he writes.

> *"Genesis teaches us several things about the image of God, what I call 'divine image bearing.' All of what we learn from the text must be accounted for in any discussion of what the image means. The Hebrew preposition translated (in) Genesis 1:26 means humankind was created (as) God's image. If we think of imaging as a verb or function, that translation makes sense. We are created to image God, to be his imagers. It is what we are by definition. The image is not an ability*

we have, but a status. We are God's representatives on Earth. To be human is to image God."

"This is why Genesis 1:26-27 is followed by what theologians call the 'dominion mandate' in verse 28. The verse informs us that God intends us to be Him on this planet. We are to create more imagers ('be fruitful and multiply... fill') in order to oversee the Earth by stewarding its resources and harnessing them for the benefit of all human imager's ('subdue... rule over')."

Notice what Dr. Heiser said. To be human is to image God. It is our status. As God's representatives we are to oversee the Earth and steward it. When man was created, he was body, soul, and spirit, and he was complete and completely human. After Adam sinned, the Light of God left man, and man's spirit became dark and incomplete. All of creation was affected by this departure of God's light. This is when Adam and Eve realized they were naked. They were no longer clothed in God's life-giving light. Ever since that day both men and women alike have been striving for completeness.

Chapter Four

God's Mandate

Earth was given to mankind. In Genesis 1:28 Adam and Eve were instructed to multiply, fill, replenish and subdue the Earth. With this mandate God gave us the ability to procreate. In fact, all of creation on Earth is able to reproduce. We must understand that the Earth was not created for the heavenly hosts. God created them before the creation of the world, and they have their own uniquely established purpose. Those angels who rebelled against God and came to Earth for their own purposes violated God's plan for them. The angels are God's heavenly family, and mankind is God's earthly family.

Fill the Earth

According to Isaiah 45:18 God created the Earth to be inhabited, and Psalm 115:16 tells us the Earth is for the children of men. It was not created to be under the rule of the devil and his kingdom of darkness. This is an important factor to understand.

> *Psalm 115:16*
> *"The heaven, even the heavens, are the Lord's, But the Earth He has given to the children of men."*

God will not violate His original mandate to mankind. Planet Earth was to be under the control of mankind not the angels according to Genesis 1:28. It is for this reason Jesus became a man. He had to become a man to take back what man (flesh) gave away. Consider this. The man, Christ Jesus, who is the second Adam, will rule in a body of flesh for eternity, and we will rule with Him.

The mandate to be fruitful and multiply and fill the earth began in the Garden of Eden. God's instructions to Adam and Eve were to fill and rule all of Eden and then extend beyond Eden throughout the entire Earth. These are the same instructions Jesus gave his disciples.

> *Acts 1:8*
> *"But you shall receive power when the Holy Spirit has come upon you; and you shall be witnesses to Me in Jerusalem, and in all Judea and Samaria, and to the end of the Earth."*

Take note of the place they were to begin - Jerusalem, the place of empowerment. The disciples were to branch out from Jerusalem and cover the whole world with the message of the New Covenant. These instructions mirror the original mandate given by God in the Garden of Eden where Adam and Eve were instructed to fill the Earth and to guard the treasure that was given. God has not given up or altered His intended purpose for man, and He will bring it to pass.

Genesis 2:15
"And the LORD God took the man, and put him into the garden of Eden to dress it and to keep it."

Strong's #H 8104 - The word "keep" in Strong's is "shamar" and means: to keep, have charge of, to guard, keep watch, watchman, protect, save life.

In like manner we have been instructed in 1 Peter 5:8.

"Be sober, be vigilant; because your adversary the devil walks about like a roaring lion, seeking whom he may devour."

Replenish the Earth

Mankind was also told to replenish the Earth. The word "replenish" has a very interesting meaning in Hebrew. Hebrew reads from right to left, and each letter has its own meaning. Something interesting is revealed in these Hebrew letters.

Strong's Concordance, #H4390, "maw-law" means Replenish/fill; To fill or be full.

The Hebrew spelling of replenish is as follows.

מ ל א (aleph) (lamed) (mem)

מ Mem - Water; massive, overpower, chaos

ל Lamed - Staff; to move in a different direction, authority, tie or bind, teach, guide, tongue

א Aleph - Ox; strength, first, power, leader

As we look at these three letters, we see the Lord intended for Adam to be much more than a gardener. Adam was created to be the leader and shepherd of the garden. He was given the strength to overpower any adversary and a staff of authority to use his words (tongue) to teach and establish what the Lord instructed. Adam was, in fact, the first shepherd.

As the first letter of the Hebrew alphabet, the letter Aleph is also prophetic in nature as is indicted by its shape. The Aleph is made up of two Hebrews letters the "Yud or Yod" and the "Vav." Note the shape of the Aleph below.

א

Yod means hand, and Vav means nail, and the Vav stands in the middle of two Yods.

The upper Yod is God's hand in heaven which is connected to the lower Yod, the hand of man (flesh) on Earth, and they are connected by a nail, the Vav. **What a beautiful picture of God and man joined together by the nail pierced hand.**

Guard Eden

Adam had a special place freely given to him, and he was instructed to be on guard. The Lord's command to guard meant more than the physical place. Adam was to guard and shepherd his family as well as all of creation. Gardens are places where plants are placed to grow and be nurtured, and we are called the planting of the Lord.

Psalm 92:12-15
"¹² The righteous shall flourish like a palm tree, He shall grow like a cedar in Lebanon.
¹³ Those who are planted in the house of the LORD shall flourish in the courts of our God
¹⁴ They shall still bear fruit in old age. They shall be fresh and flourishing,
¹⁵ To declare that the LORD is upright; He is my rock, and there is no unrighteousness in Him."

Isaiah 61:3
"That they may be called trees of righteousness, the planting of the Lord, that He may be glorified."

For an enemy to conquer any land, he must first remove the army or the "guard." This is a scriptural principle Jesus taught regarding spiritual warfare.

Mark 3:27
"²⁷ No one can enter a strong man's house and plunder his goods, unless he first binds the strong man. And then he will plunder his house."

Our adversary will use the same tactics against us. Remember, these are spiritual principles, and Satan's attacks and lies have not changed. They have been used before and will be used against us again and again, if we are not diligent to cultivate our relationship with the Lord. The adversary knows how strong you are. He knows how much time is spent in prayer and scripture reading and meditation on God's Word. He knows the loyalties of your heart and what "buttons" to push. He is looking for an entrance to make your life as ineffective as possible.

As a task master, the adversary oppresses his captives making life a tremendous burden instead of a blessing. He begins to shape our thoughts on how we view life and directs our entire focus on the present, thereby crowding out any thoughts of eternity. Satan's greatest tactic is to plant a false narrative about God. He tries to make us doubt God's goodness and faithfulness with half-truths constructed to make us feel God is withholding something good from us. This is designed to keep his captives in bondage by removing their hope.

Gideon was so beaten down, when the angel of the Lord called him a mighty man of valor that he could not believe the angel. Yet, God saw him as a mighty deliverer. Judges 6. The prophet Elijah was physically tired after his victory on Mount Carmel. However, when threatened by Jezebel, he ran away and hid in a cave and asked God to let him die. 1 Kings 18-19.

We must remember the Lord sees things much differently than we do. He is not giving us a false hope but the assurance of His council. Just follow and keep your eyes on Him. See Habakkuk 2:4, Romans 1:17, Galatians 3:11, and Hebrews 10:38 for further study.

Destiny vs Compromise

We have been given everything we need for our journey and destiny, because there is a destination and an inheritance to pursue. The assurance of God's tremendous power and authority purchased by the blood of Jesus can be ours. The liar, our adversary, will do all he can to destroy your life and make you unfruitful. He may not know your exact destiny nor your inheritance, but he is aware that every born again, child of God has within themselves the authority to conquer him as the Father has promised. In other words, you are a living threat to Satan's kingdom. All through the scriptures, in both old and new testaments, we are warned about the enemy of our soul.

Throughout church history to this present time, many believers have had a shallow understanding of the cross and blood of Jesus. In many cases this reduces the scriptures to a myth or fairy tale. Our lack of understanding of the spiritual conflict has become deadly. To some horoscopes and Ouija Boards are just games. Many see living together outside of marriage as no big deal. The list of compromises Christians make is staggering, and these compromises make us helpless and powerless against the enemy's attacks. In many ways the church has become just another social program forming God into their image instead of being transformed by the Holy Spirit into Christ's image. Our true identity and destiny can only be seen as we are transformed by the shed blood of Jesus Christ into a holy habitation full of the power and authority of God's Kingdom.

Meanwhile, the children of the adversary live and practice what they believe to full measure. They are living their lives in expectation of removing anything Christian and being free of all restraints. Over time the "church" has reduced our calling and divine purpose and relationship with God to an institutionalized, soulish knowledge of God. The term "Christian" is seen as a title given to us at natural birth. If we go to church occasionally and give an offering, that pretty much covers our duty.

When life suddenly takes a turn with sickness, disease, loss of a job or earthly possessions, or the most difficult of all, death, in many cases God is the first one to be blamed. All manner of untrue statements is spewed forth from their mouths about Him. Then God, who has such an indescribable, unmatched love for us, is viewed as an uncaring, brash tyrant.

The War is Real but Victory is Ours

Jesus has not left us to live life in the darkness of despair. He tells us plainly who we war against. We are engaged in the war of the ages, but Jesus came to destroy this destroyer of lives.

> *John 10:10*
> *"The thief does not come except to steal, and to kill, and to destroy. I have come that they may have life, and that they may have it more abundantly."*

> *1 John 3:8*
> *"He who sins is of the devil, for the devil has sinned from the beginning. For this purpose, the Son of God was manifested, that He might destroy the works of the devil."*

Those who are born of God's Spirit have entered into His victory. When we engage the adversary in the name of Jesus, we will live and overcome. We fight from a place of victory with the captain of our salvation sitting at the right hand of power. This victory is open to all who believe and continue in Him.

> *Matthew 11:12*
> *"And from the days of John the Baptist until now the kingdom of heaven suffers violence, and the violent take it by force."*

> *Jeremiah 50:25*
> *"The LORD has opened His armory, and has brought out the weapons of His indignation; For this is the work of the Lord GOD of hosts in the land of the Chaldeans."*

Satan's Tactics

Satan, or Lucifer as he is sometimes called, is a liar and a deceiver. He is our adversary and has more strength and cunning than any man or woman, which is why we need a savior. But we need to recognize that he is only a created, spiritual being limited in power and knowledge. Sometimes, the devil is depicted as a man dressed in a red suit with a pitchfork and a pointy tail with horns on his head. Others see a weak, trembling creature hiding in the corner who comes out at night to give us scary dreams. Worse yet, some say he does not exist at all but is just a made-up character created to put fear in people or to make them come to church. In some circles people make light of the devil with much bravado and laughter saying, "He may be a lion, but he just roars, because he has no teeth." This is a dangerous place to be. Jesus never took the tempter lightly, neither did Paul nor Peter. In fact, Paul instructs us to be prepared for battle.

> *Ephesians 6:10-12*
> *"[10] Finally, my brethren, be strong in the Lord and in the power of His might.*
> *[11] Put on the whole armor of God, that you may be able to stand against the wiles of the devil.*
> *[12] For we do not wrestle against flesh and blood, but against principalities, against powers, against the rulers*

of the darkness of this age, against spiritual hosts of wickedness in the heavenly places."

Peter also instructs us in 1 Peter 5:8.

"⁸ Be sober, be vigilant; because your adversary the devil walks about like a roaring lion, seeking whom he may devour."

Toothless lions do not devour. Jesus tells us Satan is a murderer capable of killing and destroying lives. The influence of this father of lies is all around us in the world and sadly even in the church. We are not engaged in a parlor game with evil. We live in a fallen world, and the battle is real and will only intensify as we approach the end of the age.

It is noteworthy to recognize that Satan has his followers. They believe he is the "good" guy and will eventually defeat Jesus in the end. His followers are engaged in all manner of sorcery, witchcraft, spellcasting, and blood sacrifice. These are not games to them. It is their form of worship, and they are serious. They see Christians as the enemy, and I think in many ways are more aware of the spiritual battle than the church. Listed below are a few names describing the devil.

Serpent (Genesis 3:1)
Adversary/Satan (Job 1)
Lucifer, meaning morning star (Isaiah 14:12)
The anointed cherub that covers (Ezekiel 28:14)
Devil/Accuser (Matthew 4:1)
Tempter (Matthew 4:3)
Ruler of the demons/ Beelzebub (Matthew 12:24)
Wicked one (Matthew 13:19)
Murderer/Father of lies (John 8:44)

God of this world (2 Corinthians 4:4)
Belial (2 Corinthians 6:15)
Prince of the power of the air (Ephesians 2:2)
Roaring lion (1 Peter 5:8)
Dragon (Revelation 12:9; 20:2)

These are not all the descriptions of our adversary, but it gives us an idea of the one we are facing. Much debate has ensued regarding the physical appearance of the devil in the garden. I offer two schools of thought on this subject from Dr. Michael Heiser in his book, *The Unseen Realm*. In Chapter 11 on page 87 he talks about the "Nachash" (the serpent) of Genesis 3.

The original Hebrew alphabet had no vowels as it consisted of only consonants. When we look at the word for serpent in Genesis 3, we see "**n-ch-sh**." If we add the vowel **"a"** in-between the consonants, we have the word "**nachash**" or "**serpent**." However, Satan is also known as the shining one, so if we add the vowels **"o"** and **"e"** in-between the consonants, then we have the word "**nochesh**" or "**the diviner**." This is one who gives information connected to the spiritual dimension.

This leads me to the conclusion that Satan was not an actual "snake" in the garden, but it was an "angelic" being who approached Eve. Both descriptions are biblical. Satan is serpentine in nature and has much knowledge of the spiritual realm. He is also cunning enough to twist God's Word to bring confusion.

When Jesus (the second Adam) was tempted in the wilderness, it paralleled the temptation in the garden. It matched the Genesis pattern of the lust of the eye, lust of the flesh, and the pride of life. It was not a "serpent" but the devil himself who tempted Jesus. In my own life I have never been tempted by a snake, but I have encountered demonic beings.

The Anointed Cherub Rebels

This ruler of fallen angels was once known as the anointed cherub. He was created before mankind and witnessed much of creation. In Job 38:7 God speaks to Job about the angels' response to creation. It says, *"The morning stars (angels) shouted for joy"* at what they witnessed. It seems as though this anointed cherub held a high place of honor among the other created angelic hosts. I would say he was as close to God as was permitted at that time.

> Ezekiel 28:14
> *"You were the anointed cherub who covers; I established you; You were on the holy mountain of God; you walked back and forth in the midst of fiery stones."*

Being the anointed cherub who "covers" would have given him firsthand knowledge of the grandeur and majesty of creation and the power of God's spoken word.

Let us review for a moment the uniqueness of mankind and how Satan responded to this knowledge. When God said in Genesis 1:28, *"Let us make man in our image and likeness and give him dominion,"* the devil knew exactly what it meant. Adam was given a kingdom with the authority to rule over it. This did not set well with the adversary. Satan's position as the anointed cherub along with the angelic hosts were as close to God as was allowed, and the position God gave man in creation put someone between the anointed cherub and God.

Furthermore, this creature of dust was given the authority to rule as God's representative on the Earth.

We do not know exactly what kind of relationship God has with angels. We do know they deliver messages, protect and intervene in this world and are an army of warriors, and they worship around the throne of God. Scripture records an account where an angel entered the camp of the Assyrians and killed 185,000 men in one night. 2 Kings 19:35. On the night Jesus was arrested, He told Peter to put his sword away, because He (Jesus) had the authority to command twelve legions of angels (approximately 80,000) to rescue Him if He so desired. Matthew 26:53. Angels are not chubby little cherubs floating on clouds. They are mighty in strength, and they obey God's command without hesitation.

Exodus 23:20-21
"[20] Behold, I send an Angel before you to keep you in the way and to bring you into the place which I have prepared.
[21] Beware of Him and obey His voice; do not provoke Him, for He will not pardon your transgressions; for My name is in Him."

One thing we do know for sure is rebellion and pride filled the anointed cherub, and he willfully rebelled against God. Satan was cast out of heaven and lost his position and intended purpose for which he was created. Ever since that moment, he has been on a mission to destroy everything God created and calls good. His main goal is to destroy God's crown of creation, mankind, and to wear it for himself. Satan saw an opportunity to gain control of God's creation with deceptive words. This is important to know as we proceed, as the power of the tongue becomes more evident.

Satan Gains Control of the Earth

The serpent knew he had to proceed with caution because of Adam's position of God-given authority and dominion over the Earth. Satan knew that a direct assault would mean certain defeat. He had already lost in his attack on God's throne. He needed another way in, and he found it with "WORDS." Let us take a look at Genesis 1:2 and what "dominion" means.

> *Strong's Hebrew Lexicon H7287 "raw-daw" - to tread down, subjugate; have dominion, prevail against, reign, rule, or rule over, take.*

When we read Genesis 3:1, we see the serpent is "**cunning**." Below is the Hebrew spelling of "cunning" and the definition of each Hebrew letter. As each letter has its own meaning, it shows us how the serpent chose his attack to do the most damage. The method used was a direct assault on the entire makeup of how Adam and Eve were created - body, soul, and spirit, (flesh, eye, life).

With the understanding of each Hebrew letter, we can then put them together to form a sentence. This will give us a deeper understanding into Satan's tactics. It is very enlightening, and I think you will find it fascinating, just as I did.

> Genesis 3:1
> *"Now the serpent was more **cunning** than any beast of the field which the LORD God had made. And he said to the woman, 'Has God indeed said, 'You shall not eat of every tree of the garden'?"* (emphasis mine)

The Hebrew rendering of the word "cunning" is as follows.

Strong's Concordance # H6191 - cunning (usually in a bad sense) crafty, prudent, subtle.

Now let us look at each Hebrew letter for cunning.

צרומ

צ Ayin – **eye**, knowledge as the eye is the window of knowledge.

ר Resh - **head of a man**, chief, top, beginning/first

ו Vav – **Nail**, to secure, join, add, **hook**

מ Mem - water, massive, overpower, **chaos**

If we put the four Hebrew letters for "cunning" into a sentence it would read - To direct the EYE to GAIN CONTROL of the HEAD, to NAIL or HOOK them to CHAOS.

I bring this out to show how the serpent deceived Eve. He made her think God was keeping some great truth from her to keep her from achieving her full potential.

This was not a straight forward physical attack against Eve. **It was simply words.** The words spoken caused her to look in a different direction to get her to think the "grass was greener on the other side." She listened, considered, and chose his reasoning. In other words, she believed the serpent was speaking truth. Just like Eve, we will trust the one whom we believe is speaking truth, and we will act accordingly.

Genesis 3:2-5
[2] And the woman said to the serpent, 'We may eat the fruit of the trees of the garden;

> ³*But of the fruit of the tree which is in the midst of the garden, God has said, 'You shall not eat it, nor shall you touch it, lest you die.'*
> ⁴*Then the serpent said to the woman, 'You will not surely die.*
> ⁵ *For God knows that in the day you eat of it your eyes will be opened, and you will be like God, knowing good and evil'."*

Jesus said in Matthew 6:22, *"The lamp of the body is the eye."* He explains this statement in verse 24 by saying there are only two masters; you either love one and hate the other or you are loyal to one and despise the other. In other words, what you see and how you see will strengthen your relationship with the master you choose to follow and obey.

This emphasizes why the Lord told Adam to **guard** the garden. How much more do those instructions apply to us today because of the deeply embedded stronghold of sin in the world?

Read the entire Matthew 6 chapter to see why this is of upmost importance.

Chapter Five

Lost Inheritance

*W*ords *matter*. We all have a thirst to build our own kingdom. This is what the adversary stimulated by his words. Yes, I mention "words" often, but words are at the heart of all creation. God SPOKE the world into existence. Every event in scripture involved WORDS. Yet, we are so blind to their power and fail to see how the adversary uses the same tactics today. His methods have not changed.

Satan is still a liar and a planter of doubt and distortion of the goodness of God. This deceiver always paints a false narrative to cause us to have a distorted view of God and His ways. A word of caution. When your adversary starts quoting God's word, it is not to edify or encourage you. His sole desire is to plant a false narrative to distort God's intended purpose in your life. The result will always be death and destruction.

Adam Kept Silent

There have been volumes written about the temptation and why Eve was chosen as the target and not Adam. Here is my quick analysis. The adversary was afraid of Adam. I base this on Genesis 1:28 where the Lord blessed Adam and Eve and placed them in the garden with the authority to rule and reign. Remember, Adam was created and given the command by God to have dominion over creation, and God did not set him up for failure. Adam had authority over anyone or anything that came into the garden, and he was instructed to guard it. This mandate to guard and to keep the garden did not come without weapons. Adam could defend Eden and defeat any adversary with his staff of authority and the power of God's Word.

God's spoken Word is our greatest weapon. Words can build up or tear down, bless or curse, bind or loose. The adversary used words to tempt Eve and gain control of this dimension. Eve was deceived as she accepted the liars' twisted reasoning and acted upon it. So, where did Adam fail? He was silent. Adam did not use the staff of authority he was given to guard the garden nor did he use the power of God's Word to bind the deceiver when he came. Adam remained silent, and sin and death entered the world.

Throughout scripture we are given instructions about our words. Our words are extremely powerful. We have the ability to create in people a life narrative of success or failure. So, why do we fail? We, like Adam, are either silent or speak out of the kingdom of darkness instead of the Kingdom of Light.

There is an interesting conversation which God had with Cain before he murdered his brother Abel in Genesis 4:7

> *"⁷ If you do well, will you not be accepted? And if you do not do well, sin lies at the door. And its desire is for you, but you should rule over it."*

I make two observations about this verse. 1) After the fall, man still had the authority to rule over sin and not be ruled by it. 2) The word "it" in some translations is "him." Cain could rule over him/sin. Either way, sin is open rebellion against God, and He expects us to resist temptation and not be controlled by it. We always have a choice. The apostle Paul writes in Romans.

> *Romans 6:11-14*
> *"¹¹ Likewise you also, reckon yourselves to be dead indeed to sin, but alive to God in Christ Jesus our Lord.*
> *¹² Therefore do not let sin reign in your mortal body, that you should obey it in its lusts.*
> *¹³ And do not present your members as instruments of unrighteousness to sin, but present yourselves to God as being alive from the dead, and your members as instruments of righteousness to God.*
> *¹⁴ For sin shall not have dominion over you, for you are not under law but under grace."*

The scripture is clear. Sin is not to be our master. By the power of the "blood of the Lamb and the word of our testimony" (Revelation 12:11) we are overcomers. We should strive to resist sin and conquer its rule in our lives. The tactics of our adversary should be quickly recognized and cast down. Realizing that walking with Jesus is not a casual call, we should be in constant fellowship with him for HE is our LIFE! As our lives are filled with His presence, we will be overcomers.

Three Areas of Temptation

Every sin committed by mankind is easily traced to three temptations, the lust of the eye, the lust of the flesh, and the pride of life. It does not matter what the sin is nor how vile it is. When we are tempted, it all goes back to these three.

> Genesis 3:6
> "So, when the woman saw that the tree was good for food, that it was pleasant to the eyes, and a tree desirable to make one wise, she took of its fruit and ate. She also gave to her husband with her, and he ate."

> 1 John 2:15-17
> "15 Do not love the world or the things in the world. If anyone loves the world, the love of the Father is not in him.
> 16 For all that is in the world—the lust of the flesh, the lust of the eyes, and the pride of life—is not of the Father but is of the world.
> 17 And the world is passing away, and the lust of it; but he who does the will of God abides forever.

Corruption of the Crown

The goal of the tempter was to take control of mankind and thereby all of creation. Since we are only complete when we are as God originally created us then anything less than what God ordained is not complete. Satan wanted Earth for his own kingdom. He was unable to usurp God's throne, so he would attempt to usurp man's authority and gain access to Kingdom Earth. In Satan's mind he would be one step closer to his ultimate goal as ruler of the heavens. The liar hoped to build a gulf so wide and deep between God and man that God would not rescue it, and thereby solidifying himself (Satan) as ruler over mankind and all creation. He succeeded and became the ruler of this world when Adam surrendered his controlling interest of Earth.

Ever since that fateful day our world has fallen to the deepest depths of depravity. We have heard statements describing people as animals, hateful, coldblooded, and so forth. Missionaries relate stories of the vileness and depravity of cultures they encounter around the world. Even seemingly civilized cultures can act and live out demonically controlled atrocities. All you have to do is look at the laws they live by, laws of suppression and brutality. How many times in history has it come to light that well-educated and outstanding citizens were found to be perpetrators of horrendous crimes leaving their communities speechless? It is obvious these are not Godly characteristics but satanic in origin. Therefore, if God is not present in a person's life, they are incomplete and unholy.

Only Complete in Him

Our only hope to be complete is in Jesus. When God created Adam in the flesh, he was complete, and God said, *"It is good."* God has a purpose for the Earth and mankind <u>in our flesh</u>. You see, God has a destiny for you and me, and our flesh is a perfect fit to fulfill all He created us to be and do on Earth. Does that seem strange to you? Consider this. Jesus took on a body of flesh. He was resurrected and returned to heaven in a body of flesh and bone. God in Jesus Christ has chosen to live in a fleshly body for all eternity here on Earth in order to fellowship with us. Emmanuel, God with us.

Remember, God created this Earth to be inhabited forever, and God's plan is for His children to rule and reign with Him. We can only do that if we are "one" with the Father in His purposes. John's gospel chapter 17 records Jesus' prayer to His Father before going to the cross. There Jesus prays for His disciples and for all those who would come to salvation. In this passage we see the ultimate goal of the Father's heart for you and me which is to become one with Him and with one another. John 17:3 says eternal life is found only in knowing God.

John 17:3 and 21

"³ And this is eternal life, that they may know You, the only true God, and Jesus Christ whom You have sent."

"²¹ 'That they all may be one as You, Father, are in Me, and I in You; that they also may be one in Us, that the world may believe that You sent Me'."

This is the ultimate joining of God to His creation through the blood of His covenant. In this way we may become partakers of His divine nature. II Peter 1:2-4. Yes, He alone is the King of Kings and Lord of Lords. Yet, He has invited us to be the kings and lords over this Earth with Him as the ultimate King and Lord over all.

This position of authority is not automatic. We must enter into life through Christ Jesus and be transformed by Him. This involves a journey with choices if we want to live as His special people on the Earth. It is the putting off of our old sinful ways and a putting on of a life renewed by the Spirit of God. It is a daily process of spending time with Jesus.

Colossians 2:8-15
"⁸ Beware lest anyone cheat you through philosophy and empty deceit, according to the tradition of men, according to the basic principles of the world, and not according to Christ.
⁹ For in Him dwells all the fullness of the Godhead bodily;
¹⁰ and you are complete in Him, who is the head of all principality and power.
¹¹ In Him you were also circumcised with the circumcision made without hands, by putting off the body of the sins of the flesh, by the circumcision of Christ,
¹² buried with Him in baptism, in which you also were raised with Him through faith in the working of God, who raised Him from the dead.
¹³ And you, being dead in your trespasses and the uncircumcision of your flesh, He has made alive together with Him, having forgiven you all trespasses,
¹⁴ having wiped out the handwriting of requirements that was against us, which was contrary to us. And He has taken it out of the way, having nailed it to the cross.
¹⁵ Having disarmed principalities and powers, He made a public spectacle of them, triumphing over them in it."

What man became after the fall is lived out in actions and words according to the nature of the ruling authority on Earth. The weapon the liar used in his attack was "words" spoken to Eve to plant a false narrative. It worked then, and it still works today.

I would say the greatest area of our spiritual blindness and ignorance is in our speech. This is a stronghold in the lives of many with devastating results. How many "words" are at the back of all the anger and hatred and wars in the world resulting in the destruction of so many lives and nations? Many will say, "No one tells me what to do." This is another deception. We all live under the authority of a kingdom, God's or Satan's, and our lives produce the fruit of the kingdom in which we live.

We all know the verse, *"Your kingdom come, your will be done on Earth as it is in heaven."* Matthew 6:10; Luke 11:2. This is not only the cry of those who are believers but the heart cry of many whose lives are bound in darkness. People may seem confident outwardly, but in the stillness of the night when no one is around and the brokenness and emptiness of existence is screaming at them, they hunger and thirst for true freedom. We all long for someone greater to give purpose and meaning to this life.

The character and tactics of the adversary were on full display in the garden with Adam and Eve. Satan achieved his immediate goal of death and destruction. The perversion of mankind seemed to have won the day. But wait, the Lord God of Heaven has a plan.

Salvation's Journey Begins

God's Response. The journey of cleansing the temple began in the Garden of Eden. The sacrifice God made in the garden on behalf of Adam and Eve was just the beginning of a journey with many sacrifices and altars. There would be a Tabernacle, mercy seat, lampstand, table of shewbread and many other articles used. Two temples would be built over time, all revealing a wonderful plan of grace, mercy, longsuffering and our ultimate adoption back into the family of God.

In the garden, after the willful sin of Adam, the Lord put a plan of salvation into motion that was planned before the foundation of the world. We do not know the nature of what departed from Adam and Eve at the fall, but I believe it was the presence of God's Spirit of Life and Light. John 1:4. Darkness did not drive out the Light. Darkness can never drive out light. When man made his choice, the Light voluntarily left. It was evident Adam and Eve wanted control of their lives on their own terms. Consequently, the coldness and darkness of death and fear became their master just as God said would happen.

Coverings of Fig Leaves

Adam and Eve's reaction to cover themselves was immediate, and their choice of garment came from a fig tree. This put into motion a fruitless, spiritual tree grown from a spiritual mountain that would rule over them. All of the characteristics of that mountain were free to reproduce in them. It does not matter how beautifully tailored the fig leaves are or how compelling our excuses may be. The adversary will try to convince us our fig leaves are adequate. However, our best efforts are not acceptable garments for the presence of God and His righteousness. They just do not work. We are still exposed and destined for the coldness and darkness of fear and death and complete separation from God.

In Genesis 3:9-21 the Lord pronounced judgement on all the participants. However, God did not clothe Adam and Eve until they had been confronted with their disobedience. Even with their excuses they were brought face to face with their sin, and they had to witness the severity of their actions in the death of an innocent animal. The scripture does not tell us what kind of animal was sacrificed, but we can assume it was a lamb for in the future lambs were the acceptable sacrifice. In like manner, we can only be clothed in the righteousness of Jesus by confessing our sin and openly receiving Him. Only then can we be washed in the blood of the perfect sacrifice, the Lamb of God.

Genesis 3:21
"²¹ Also for Adam and his wife the Lord God made tunics of skin, and clothed them."

In receiving the covering provided by the Lord God, Adam and Eve confessed their disobedience and acknowledged that the lamb died in their place. In this action the Lord God performed the first blood sacrifice and established a precedent for mankind to follow. Only a perfect unblemished lamb could atone for their act of disobedience.

Think of all the effort mankind has put forth to have fellowship with God. Yet, the blood sacrifice only covered their sins for one year and had to be repeated year after year. This is a constant reminder we are sinners, and the cycle is never ending. Adam and Eve and countless generations thereafter were willing to embrace this blood covenant with God, because they so desperately wanted to gain back what was lost in fellowship with their maker. Because man's value is so great God performed this first sacrifice and then **became** the last sacrifice on the cross. By His death Jesus established a New and Better Covenant. See Hebrews 8:6.

Was Satan Surprised?

I do not think this action by God on behalf of Adam and Eve was the expected response the adversary was counting on. Remember, he permanently lost his place as the anointed cherub when he rebelled. What he thought God would do is anyone's guess. He understood and had experienced the holiness of God first hand. In God's holiness Satan knows rebellion is dealt with swiftly and without mercy. At least this had been his experience, and Satan may have expected God to do the same with Adam. But the Lord had another plan.

Our God was very much aware that these things would take place before anything was created, and He was prepared. When we read Genesis 1, we see the phrase "God said" throughout the entire chapter. In Genesis 2:4 we are introduced to an additional name for God - LORD.

Dr. Michael Lake in his book, *The Shinar Directive*, on pages 38-40 writes the following.

> *"In Genesis 2, God reveals Himself for the first time as the LORD GOD (YHVH-Elohim). YHVH is considered in Scripture as the most sacred name of God. When God began dealing with mankind, He revealed part of His nature that Lucifer had never seen. Let us look at what the rabbis understand about God as YHVH-Elohim.*
>
> *"The divine appellation Elohim, translated 'God,' was understood to denote His aspect of judgement and YHVH, translated "Lord," His aspect of mercy. In the creation of mankind, God balanced mercy and judgment together. This is very significant, and it took Lucifer by surprise."*

We can also see this in the meaning of the Hebrew letters for YHVH reading from right to left.

יהוה

Yod - hand
Hey - behold, reveal, window
Vav - nail
Hey - behold, reveal, window

We see here in the name LORD that God revealed His plan beforehand. "Behold the Hand. Behold the Nail" or "Behold the nail pierced hand." Remember the Aleph א in chapter 4? Our Lord God identified with mankind in eternity past and purposed beforehand to become the Savior of all that was lost.

His name is not only God (Elohim) but Lord God (YHVH Elohim). God's justice is revealed in the name translated "God" which is all Satan knew. But in His name "Lord God" the **Mercy and Justice** of the creator are joined together. Praise the Lord!

We need to understand that the Lord God is not haphazard or cold in His dealings with mankind. He extends abundant grace to everyone who comes. This grace is not only for salvation but also becomes a precious gift of teaching and spiritual instruction on how to live.

> *Titus 2:11-15*
> *"11 For the grace of God that brings salvation has appeared to all men,*
> *12 teaching us that, denying ungodliness and worldly lusts, we should live soberly, righteously, and godly in the present age,*

> [13] *looking for the blessed hope and glorious appearing of our great God and Savior Jesus Christ,*
> [14] *who gave Himself for us, that He might redeem us from every lawless deed and purify for Himself His own special people, zealous for good works."*

God's Plan for You

Our Lord has a distinct plan for each of us, and it is good and involves His only begotten son, Jesus Christ. Galatians 4:4 tells us that when the fullness of time came, the Lord God sent His son. In Christ's willful sacrifice we are now able to be free from the power of sin over our lives.

> *Hebrews 10:16-18*
> *"*[16] *'This is the covenant that I will make with them after those days, says the LORD: I will put My laws into their hearts, and in their minds, I will write them,'*
> [17] *then He adds, 'Their sins and their lawless deeds I will remember no more.'*
> [18] *Now where there is remission of these, there is no longer an offering for sin."*

We are beginning to see clues of God's overall plan for the redemption of mankind and the creation. He first spoke in Genesis 1:3, *"Let there be light, and there was light."* In this declaration light appeared and drove out the darkness and prepared the way for the establishment of everything needed to sustain life. Jesus said in John 14:6, *"I am the way, the truth and the life. No man comes unto the Father except by Me."* In this same way the Holy Spirit moves into our darkness to prepare us for life. The spoken Word of God, anointed and empowered, brings conviction. When repentance follows, death and darkness are driven out. This is being born again or as some say, born of the Spirit of God. 2 Corinthians 5:17 says it this way. *"Therefore, if anyone is in Christ, he is a new creation; old things have passed away; behold, all things have become new."*

Chapter Six

Deliverance from Bondage

A Short History Lesson. The latter chapters of the book of Genesis records the history of the descendants of Abraham's grandson, Jacob, whose name was changed to Israel by the Angel of the Lord. Seventy members of Jacob's family went into Egypt because of a famine in the land of Canaan. Now Canaan was the land which God had promised to give Abraham as an inheritance. The land was called Canaan then, but it is the same land we know today as Israel. After the famine ended, they did not go back to their promised land but remained in the land of Egypt. They had grown comfortable in Egypt and saw no reason to return. As a result, they took on the mind set and attitudes of the Egyptians. They were living among pagans who eventually began to persecute them. Because they had grown so many in number, the Egyptians put the Israelites into bondage and made them their slaves.

Four hundred years later Jacob's descendants were living as slaves in a land not their own. Their bondage had become a way of life all the while desiring freedom. They remembered the promise God made to their father, Abraham, to give them a homeland, and they cried out for a deliverer. The book of Exodus in the Bible records the details around the Jewish people's deliverance from slavery and bondage. This has become known as The Exodus.

As we look at their exodus from Egypt, we see the Lord God revealed as their deliverer. Moses was the man God used to confront Pharaoh to free the people. Through Moses the Lord God revealed His plan and purpose for His people and invited them to participate in the journey out of bondage into their promised inheritance.

Moses is a picture of another deliverer, Jesus Christ, whom the Lord God would send to free all people from the bondage of sin and death. God promised Abraham that all the nations on Earth would be blessed through his Seed. This is the reason God called Abraham out in order to establish his descendants on Earth as His own special people. The Lord is the one who empowers His people to be all they were created to be. It may be helpful to look at a verse from Exodus 20:2 and Deuteronomy 5:6. These verses are identical, so I will only list one.

> Exodus 20:2
> "I am the LORD your God, who brought you out of the land of Egypt, out of the house of bondage."

In chapter 5 we saw how God identified Himself in Genesis 2:4 as the **Lord God**. In Exodus 3:14 He reveals Himself as **"I Am the Lord God."** He is one and the same from the beginning. He is both Creator and Deliverer.

The Genesis' Hebrew-Chaldee Lexicon says; I (ever) shall be (the same) that I am (today)- eternal and immutable, who will never be other than the same.

You may ask, "What does this have to do with Jesus cleansing the temple and cursing the fig tree in Matthew 21?" It might surprise you, but the book of Exodus reveals that God has a destiny and an inheritance for His people. The Lord made a promise to Abraham that his descendants would inherit the land of Canaan, and the Lord would fulfill His promise. However, it would require the participation of the Israelites who were still in bondage. They were never destined to be slaves but a kingdom of priests to the Lord God.

In like manner we were not created to live as slaves bound in chains of sin. Just as Israel was destined for greatness before the Lord, so are all who are born of the Spirit of God. There is a journey to a destination that awaits each of us, and it will require us to become participants in His plan.

Types and Shadows

There are many types and shadows in the scriptures, and these analogies help us understand God's love and plan for us. One type was the Temple, the physical structure to house God's presence, and it helps us to understand how the Lord loves us and desires to fill us with His Spirit and to make us His holy habitation.

In Exodus 20:2 the Lord God declared that He is the one who brought them up out of the land of Egypt, the house of bondage. In the spiritual sense Egypt is a type of the world, and Satan is the god of this world. Yet, Pharaoh and the Egyptians were not so eager to give up their slaves. Why should they? So, God sent ten plagues upon the land of Egypt to demonstrate His power to deliver His people. This established fear in the Egyptians, but it gave hope to God's people.

> *Exodus 12:12*
> *"^{12} 'For I will pass through the land of Egypt on that night, and will strike all the firstborn in the land of Egypt, both man and beast; and against all the gods of Egypt I will execute judgment: I am the L ORD."*

On the following page is a list of the gods judged in Egypt during the ten plagues.

Zondervanacademic.com

Nile to blood	Hapi (also called Apis), the bull god, god of the Nile; Isis, goddess of the Nile; Khnum, ram god, guardian of the Nile; others
Frogs	Heqet, goddess of birth, with a frog head
Gnats	Set, god of the desert storms
Flies	Re, a sun god; Uatchit, possibly represented by the fly
Death of livestock	Hathor, goddess with a cow head; Apis, the bull god, symbol of fertility
Boils	Sekhmet, goddess with power over disease; Sunu, the pestilence god; Isis, healing goddess
Hail	Nut, the sky goddess; Osiris, god of the crops and fertility; Set, god of the desert storms
Locusts	Nut, the sky goddess; Osiris, god of the crops and fertility
Darkness	Re, the sun god; Horus, a sun god; Nut, a sky goddess; Hathor, a sky goddess
Death of firstborn	Min, god of reproduction; Heqet, goddess who attended women at childbirth; Isis, goddess who protected children; Pharaoh's firstborn son considered a god

Why am I rehearsing the events of the Exodus and the plagues over Egypt? Because Egypt was the world power of its day, but God brought it to utter ruin. God displayed His authority and power in Egypt over every demonic power in creation. Each plague showed the Lord God's authority over the demon gods of Egypt. Make no mistake. We are facing spiritual powers of darkness today, and we can observe their manifesting control in the lives of many.

These so-called gods are the fallen angels who followed the anointed cherub into rebellion against the Lord God. They are limited in power yet have their own "false narratives" of deception to propel the human race deeper into darkness away from their Creator. At first glance they may seem benevolent, but in actuality these gods demanded the allegiance of human sacrifices for any favor they may or may not dispose.

The Lord God simply asked the Israelites to sacrifice a lamb and put the blood on the door post and lintel of their houses. But there is more to this story than first meets the eye. This was an act of faith. They had to act on faith that what Moses told them was true. Remember, they lived in a land of pagan gods with all types of ritualistic activity all around. They had cried out for over four hundred years to be free, and now, instead of fighting, all they had to do was walk in obedience and sacrifice a lamb and put its blood on the doorpost. Their faith in the Word of God through Moses was being tested, and I am sure they were a little fearful. Initially, when Moses first returned to Egypt to confront Pharaoh, their burdens had intensified. They had already witnessed nine plagues, and their circumstance was not any better. Are we sure this is what God wants us to do?

Onward to Our Inheritance

Shut in with God. Maybe you have received a word from the Lord in your heart, and your expectations have risen, but the answer seems delayed. Many times, the adversary will taunt you and endeavor to sow words of doubt just as he did with Eve in the garden. So, what should you do? The same thing the Israelite people did. Enter through the blood covered door and SHUT it! The adversary cannot enter where the blood is applied.

Shut yourself in with God and feast on His Word and His promises. Get alone with Him in prayer. You may hear the sounds and threats of the adversary, but he cannot enter your space unless you allow him. The amount of authority you have and walk in will always be according to the time spent in the presence of the Lord and His Word. The instruction to shut the door occurs in many places throughout scripture. When we go to prayer, Jesus instructs us to shut the door to the prayer room. Matthew 6:6.

Putting the blood over the door was an outward expression of simple faith, for they were yet to meet the Lord God as their deliverer. The Israelites only knew about God from the stories passed down through generations. When Moses informed them that he had met God at a burning bush, they believed the Lord God had visited the children of Israel and remembered their affliction, and they bowed their heads and worshipped. Desiring to be free from the bondage of slavery, they acted in simple faith on Moses' words. They believed God had heard their cry for freedom and brought them a deliverer. In their simple step of obedience, they distanced ourselves from the ways of Egypt. What they were doing had never been done before. This was a new way. In like manner, we are to live our lives in a way that is different from the world.

> *2 Corinthians 6:17*
> *"Therefore, "Come out from among them and be separate, says the Lord. Do not touch what is unclean, And I will receive you."*

Just as Moses was sent back into Egypt to deliver God's chosen people, Jesus was sent into the world as the Lamb of God to deliver all who believe and to transform them into a holy habitation for His presence.

Just Compromise

Before the final plague that forced Pharaoh to release the children of Israel, there had been many destroying plagues over the land of Egypt by God's hand, and each time Pharaoh hardened his heart. After the eighth plague of locust with even more devastating results, Pharaoh was ready to offer a compromise. Pharaoh would allow the men to go out into the wilderness to sacrifice, but they had to leave the women and children behind. Moses refused the offer, and God brought the ninth plague of total darkness over the land of Egypt for three days. Once more Pharaoh offered a compromise. Every man, woman and child would be allowed to go, but they would have to leave their livestock in Egypt. Moses answered, "Not a hoof shall be left behind," resulting in the tenth and final plague, the death of the firstborn of Egypt. Exodus 10:26.

The tempter will always offer compromise. Compromise is intended to keep you connected to the familiar, even if it is bondage. It is possible to stay tethered to our past, but that means the adversary remains in control of our thoughts and actions which can only breed discouragement and a fruitless life. Is this what you want? I certainly do not. It is a miserable place to be and a miserable way to live.

Let us Break Free

Breaking free of the chains of bondage that kept God's people from their divine purpose is what redemption is all about. The same is true for you and me. It is the only way to become a holy habitation for God's presence and a kingdom of priests fit for our destined purpose.

Psalm 105:37 tells us that not one feeble person was among the Israelites when they left Egypt. The word feeble means to lack strength in the legs or ankles. God performed a complete healing in their physical bodies as well in their spirits that day. As they walked in obedience to apply the blood of the lamb as instructed, something supernatural happened. Their spiritual eyes were opened by hope, their faith soared, and they were made physically strong for the journey out of Egypt.

Whose Voice do you Hear?

Spiritual vision and hearing as well as physical vision and hearing are a must on this journey. The god of this world gains control of our minds and thought processes through our eyes and ears and our imaginations. When we listen to Satan's voice and speak his lies instead of listening to God's voice and speaking His truth, we begin to stumble. The

Israelites would face many moments of destiny along the way to prepare them for their destination. How they responded during their journey would reveal if they were walking as God's special people or if they were still in bondage to the ways and desires of Egypt.

The Lord was preparing them to be something special. He wanted the Israelites to become a living testimony to the world of God's compassion and power to deliver. As they began their journey, I am sure each person had a mental picture of what the land flowing with milk and honey would look like. They were now free of the toils of slavery, and everyone was rejoicing. But it didn't take long for fear to creep into their minds. Yes, they were free to go and live as God's people, but the journey ahead would require a dying to the old ways of thinking and speaking.

The breaking free from the house of bondage, the removal of fruitless fig trees and the confronting of the mountain from which it grew would begin very soon. Our journey out of bondage in many ways parallels the journey of the Israelites out of their bondage.

They would accuse God of bringing them into the wilderness to die, and that is true. God desired their slave-bondage mentality to die, so His life and purpose could be birthed in them. We are no different. What we imagine our journey to be and the reality of the journey are very different. Facing the ingrained strongholds of the god of this world may seem like a daunting, impossible task. The snares they faced are the same we face today. We think we have to do this by our own strength, but that is a lie from the established mountain. God has brought you to this place to learn and grow in relationship with Him.

Stepping into the Unknown

The Israelites had limited understanding at the time. They failed to understand what the journey of moving from Egypt to the Promised Land would entail. It would be a journey to prepare them to take possession of their inheritance. Many moments of "destiny" would be faced, as the Lord knew there would be trials and tests along the way. What they needed most was a change in their way of thinking. The Israelites were not prepared nor did they understand what taking their inheritance would require of them. The Lord always does the heavy lifting for us, but He requires us to actively participate in the process of being changed. The Lord God gently and graciously led the Israelites on an easy path. He does the same for us.

> *Exodus 13:17*
> *"17 Then it came to pass, when Pharaoh had let the people go, that God did not lead them by way of the land of the Philistines, although that was near for God said, 'Lest perhaps the people change their minds when they see war, and return to Egypt'."*

There are many "moments of destiny" on our journey to our destination and inheritance. These moments will reveal what needs to be laid aside so Christ can be formed in us.

The Enemy's Strongholds

For over four hundred years Israel's enemies had put down roots, built large cities, and multiplied in number in the land promised to Abraham. The Lord promised to give Abraham's descendants this land, but it would require participation in the battle on their part.

From the many sources I have read, Israel reached the Jordan river, the entrance to their destination and inheritance, approximately one and a half to two years after leaving Egypt. During that time Moses received the Law, and they built the Tabernacle with all its furniture. They were also taught the proper way to worship, serve, and honor the Lord. In addition, they received a civil law. All of this was needed in order to conquer and prosper in the land. This was God's allotted time for them to grow from knowing about Him and His acts, to **knowing Him and living in His ways.**

This is the warring of two kingdoms. God had already delivered them from the gods of Egypt, but these gods were connected to the powers that were now occupying the "Promise Land." God's people at that time failed to cast off their slave, bondage mentality. The result was when they faced the fortified city of Jericho (The Mountain), they believed what they saw (eye gate). Their fear said, "Jericho could not be destroyed." They looked at their own strength and not God's.

All along their journey they were faced, time and time again, with how much of Egypt they still had in themselves. Each time they faced a crisis, instead of seeking the Lord and growing in the strength of His might, they chose to depend on their own resources and abilities. They would even desire to go back to Egypt to the place of their captivity. They longingly remembered the food and the familiar, forgetting they were slaves and the hardships they faced there. This lifestyle mindset was predictable. Through no fault of their own, they were born slaves. It was all they knew. It would take time to change their desires and ways of thinking.

We are no different. Being born into sin and held in bondage, when freedom comes, we know nothing about this new life nor how to live it. How often are we like the Israelites and fail to fully appreciate this new life of the Spirit and the benefits that are part of being chosen by God? When difficult times come, it is easier to long for the familiar and to act or react in the way we always have. God invites us to participate in the establishing of His Kingdom on Earth. Let us not draw back in fear. I do not write these things to be critical of Israel's response in their own destiny moments. We are so much like them. The apostle Paul writes.

1 Corinthians 10:11
"Now all these things happened to them as examples, and they were written for our admonition, upon whom the ends of the ages have come."

This journey was their destiny to prepare them for the destination ahead and their promised inheritance. The Lord intentionally lead them in the way that would best teach them to look to Him as their source. The Red Sea crossing, the bitter waters of Marah, the bread from heaven, and much more. Every part of the journey was designed to change their slave mentality to a priestly, holy minded people ready to establish God's Kingdom on the Earth.

Each trial they faced was for the purpose of strengthening them for their destination. Facing fruitless fig trees is not pleasant, because it reveals which kingdom, we are drawing our life from. Do we remove it or embrace it? We cannot be neutral. A decision must be made, and **now** is the appointed time. We will not advance until it is removed. It is our choice to make. Facing the unproductive areas of our life begins with conviction, and that can be painful.

The Psalmist wrote in Psalm 119:71-75 of being afflicted and said it was good. I realize this is not a popular statement, but let us take a moment and see what he said.

Psalm 119:71-75
"71 It is good for me that I have been afflicted,
that I may learn Your statutes.
72 The law of Your mouth is better to me
than thousands of coins of gold and silver.
73 Your hands have made me and fashioned me;
give me understanding, that I may learn Your
commandments.
74 Those who fear You will be glad when they see me,
Because I have hoped in Your word.
75 I know, O Lord, that Your judgments are right,
And that in faithfulness You have afflicted me."

The word "afflicted" in *Strong's Concordance #H6031* is "aw-naw" and means *"to be occupied, be busied with, to afflict, to oppress, humble, and be bowed down."*

The Psalmist is saying that he was grateful for his affliction for his eyes were opened to see what had occupied his life, so it could be removed and replaced with fruitfulness. We are to rejoice when our eyes are opened, because deliverance is offered and is possible.

James 1:2-3
"2 My brethren, count it all joy when you fall into
various trials,
3 knowing that the testing of your faith produces
patience."

As we move forward in our journey, we must realize that when Jesus freed us and set us on this journey, His intention was for us to enter the fight of faith, advance the Kingdom of God, and occupy until He comes. Our fight is with the kingdom of darkness, not our brothers and sisters in Christ.

According to Hebrews 4, when the Israelites refused to cross the Jordan River to fight the giants in the land, the Lord's anger was stirred up against them. As a result, He swore in His wrath they would not enter His rest. This happened because of their unbelief. That generation wondered in the wilderness for forty years all because of fear of failure. How often do we miss out on a miracle of God's deliverance, because we are afraid to step out in obedience?

Destiny Moments

Below, I have listed four words and their definitions which I believe are important to our understanding of our journey from slavery to a life of ruling and reigning as God's people. Every adult twenty years and older missed their appointed time because of fear, doubt and unbelief.

> *Numbers 14:29*
> *"The carcasses of you who have murmured against Me shall fall in this wilderness, ...according to your entire number, from twenty years old and above."*

The same can be true of us if we are not careful. Just because something has been promised does not mean it will automatically come to pass. If old attitudes and godless traditions of the past are not cast off, the promise may go unfulfilled. That was not and is not God's plan for us. Just as the Israelites had to choose to die to self and their old ways in order to conquer, so must we. Those who leave the past behind and embrace the promise will live the promise.

Webster's New World College Dictionary

> **Journey** – (1) the act or an instance of traveling from one place to another; trip (2) any course or passage from one stage or experience to another.
>
> **Destiny** – (1) the seemingly or inevitable or <u>necessary succession of events</u> (2) what will necessarily happen to any person or thing (one's) fate (3) that which determines events; said of either a supernatural agency or necessity.
>
> **Destination**- settlement, appointment, (1) a destining or being destined (2) the end for which something or someone is destined, (3) <u>the place</u> toward which someone or something is going or sent.
>
> **Inheritance** – (1) the action of inheriting (2) something inherited or to be inherited; legacy; bequest (3) ownership by birthright; right to inherit (4) anything received as if by inheritance from a predecessor (5) any characteristic passed on by heredity.

Everyone is on the journey called life. Our lives have a beginning date and an ending date, and we relate to it by time. How often do we say or hear things like, "I have an appointment," or "I'll deal with that later."? Time and appointments control our lives much more than we realize, and in each of these appointments we are faced with choices. I call "choices" **destiny** moments. We are faced with them every day, and the choice we make, at any given moment, will have an impact on our lives whether great or small, good or bad. Every choice we make sets a pattern which, over time, we will identify with.

God brought Israel out of the land of Egypt which is a type of salvation, and He delivered them from the house of bondage. Still, many remained in bondage, because Egypt had enslaved their minds and had controlled how they functioned each day for so long. Their way of thinking and how they responded to life needed to be changed. They had a destination and an inheritance to enter into, and it would require heaven's strategies and authority to be fulfilled.

The ways of bondage and Egypt are allies with the powers of darkness which have taken what is rightfully yours. Coming into agreement with God's ways and His finished work is the only way to take your own promise land. You and I are on a journey to our inheritance. Embrace your journey. Embrace your destiny. Your destination will require this, if you want to receive your inheritance.

Engaging

the

Plan

Matthew 21:12-22

"¹² Then Jesus went into the temple of God and drove out all those who bought and sold in the temple, and overturned the tables of the moneychangers and the seats of those who sold doves.

¹³ And He said to them, "It is written, 'My house shall be called a house of prayer,' but you have made it a 'den of thieves.'"

¹⁴ Then the blind and the lame came to Him in the temple, and He healed them.

¹⁵ But when the chief priests and scribes saw the wonderful things that He did, and the children crying out in the temple and saying, "Hosanna to the Son of David!" they were indignant

¹⁶ and said to Him, "Do You hear what these are saying?" And Jesus said to them, "Yes. Have you never read, 'Out of the mouth of babes and nursing infants You have perfected praise'?"

¹⁷ Then He left them and went out of the city to Bethany, and He lodged there.

¹⁸ Now in the morning, as He returned to the city, He was hungry.

¹⁹ And seeing a fig tree by the road, He came to it and found nothing on it but leaves, and said to it, "Let no fruit grow on you ever again." Immediately the fig tree withered away.

²⁰ And when the disciples saw it, they marveled, saying, "How did the fig tree wither away so soon?"

²¹ So Jesus answered and said to them, "Assuredly, I say to you, if you have faith and do not doubt, you will not only do what was done to the fig tree, but also if you say to this mountain, 'Be removed and be cast into the sea,' it will be done.

²² And whatever things you ask in prayer, believing, you will receive."

Chapter Seven

Cleansing the Temple

*J*esus *arrives in Jerusalem.* Before going to the cross, Jesus must first accomplish three things. He must cleanse the Temple, curse the fig tree, and remove the mountain stronghold. Matthew 21:12-22 records Jesus' last week on Earth before His crucifixion. On the first day of the last week, Jesus cleansed the Temple, God's house, by driving out the moneychangers. The next day Jesus came upon a fig tree without any fruit and cursed the tree and the mountain from which it grew. It may be easy for us to understand why Jesus cleansed the Temple because of the corruption. However, it is probably not as easy to understand why Jesus cursed the fig tree. Everything I have written up to this point has been to prepare you for a deeper understanding into our study of Matthew 21. By now you should be getting a better picture of why Jesus cleansed the Temple and cursed the fig tree. If not, you will soon.

Jesus rode into Jerusalem on a donkey that first day of the week, and a multitude of people went before Him with shouts of "Hosanna to the Son of David!" Immediately after this scene Jesus went into the Temple of God. What He finds there stirs up a holy zeal within Him, and He displays His passion for His Father's house. Jesus drove out all those who bought and sold in the Temple, and He overturned the tables of the moneychangers and the seats of those who sold doves.

It must be remembered that everything Jesus did in the physical world was an indication to what He would do in the spiritual realm. Jesus' actions at the Temple on that first day and His actions the very next day when He cursed the fig tree were a declaration. His actions were prophetic in nature declaring that the kingdom of darkness would soon to be destroyed. However, the uprooting of Satan's power would come at the cost of the death, burial and resurrection of Jesus Christ. Let us take a look at an interesting event that took place which shows that <u>everything</u> Jesus did leading up to His death was significant.

> Luke 9:30-31
> "³⁰ And behold, two men talked with Him, who were Moses and Elijah,
> ³¹ who appeared in glory and spoke of His decease which He was about to accomplish at Jerusalem."

The importance of this verse is found in the word "accomplish."

> Strong's Concordance #G4137
> to make full, to fill up, i.e. fill to the brim; to render full, to cause to abound, to furnish or supply liberally; I abound, I am liberally supplied; i.e. to complete to fill to the top: so that nothing shall be wanting, to full measure.

When we think of the death and resurrection of Jesus, we think of salvation and the removal of the penalty for sin. Jesus must satisfy the holiness of the Father completely. The darkness of sin is impossible to grasp with our mortal understanding for this is spirit. The apostle Paul tells us in 1 Timothy 6:16, *"God alone has immortality, dwelling in unapproachable light."* Not one part of the holy requirement could be left undone. To be honest we cannot comprehend the magnitude of God's holiness. Jesus came to remove everything that hinders us from approaching the throne of God.

We need a full understanding of why it was necessary for Jesus to cleanse the Temple in Jerusalem. The Jewish religious leaders at this point in history were completely out of touch with God's heart of redemption. Jesus wanted His disciples to know that this is not the way to true worship. Time was short, and He needed to show them what mattered most to the Father.

Darkness in the Temple

The Ark of the Covenant (Mercy Seat) had not been in the Holy of Holies for several hundred years. The Ark is last mentioned in 2 Chronicles chapter 35. Tradition says the prophet, Jeremiah, took the Ark and hid it in a cave on Mt. Nebo, but no one knows for sure. It is hidden somewhere, and it has been debated by scholars for many years where it might be. The point is this. The Jewish people were worshipping and sacrificing lambs but did not have the Ark of the Covenant on which to place the blood of the sacrificed animals on the Day of Atonement.

> Matthew 21:12-13
> "*¹² Then Jesus went into the temple of God and drove out all those who bought and sold in the temple, and overturned the tables of the moneychangers and the seats of those who sold doves.*
> *¹³ And He said to them, "It is written, 'My house shall be called a house of prayer,' but you have made it a den of thieves."*

Notice two phrases in this verse – first, "My house" and second, "den of thieves." Jesus was talking about His Temple and what it had become. With the Ark of the Covenant missing they did not have the light of God's presence. By design there was no artificial light in the Holy of Holies. Only the light of the glory of God could illuminate that space. So, darkness ruled in the heart of the Temple. An empty Holy of Holies corresponds to the heart of man without the presence of God in which case darkness rules.

The priests began to fill the void with what they considered holy. It was a redefining and an adding to the Book of the Law. This made the priesthood and worship something to be bought and sold. As for the moneychangers, only Temple coins were accepted, and all foreign currency had to be converted. The exchange rate was controlled by greedy men, and as a result, abuse of the poor was common place.

The Court of the Gentiles had been turned into a barnyard, crowding out Gentile worshipers. They had no place to go, and if they entered the Outer Court, they would be killed for defiling the Temple. The Court of the Gentiles had been set up so the nations could come into a relationship with God. Profit, status, and self-interest controlled the atmosphere around the Temple, and Passover was sure to bring in huge profits.

The Temple Compound

The Temple compound should have been used to bring all people to a knowledge of God, Jews and Gentiles alike. Its design mirrored God's original mandate to fill the Earth with His presence beginning with Eden and then extending throughout the whole Earth. We can see this in the design of the Temple compound which consisted of four separate areas.

> 1. **The Court of the Priests,** which was the temple structure itself with the Holy Place and all of its furnishings plus the Holy of Holies
> 2. **The Court of Israel**, for men only
> 3. **The Outer Court**, the court of the women
> 4. **The Court of the Gentiles**

The temple compound can also be seen as a prophetic picture of the church and its mission. Jesus commanded his disciples in Acts 1:8 to wait for the Holy Spirit to be endued with power to be witnesses in…

> 1 - Jerusalem (The Court of the Priests)
> 2 - Judea (The Court of Israel)
> 3 - Samaria (The Outer Court)
> 4 - To all the Earth (The Court of the Gentiles)

Yet, legalism was the order of the day, and it was an offence to the God of mercy and compassion. The religious system during Jesus' time had removed all semblance of the true nature and heart of the Father and had replaced it with a merit system of worship, and Jesus confronted them about it.

> *Mark 7:6-9 and 13*
> *⁶ "Well did Isaiah prophesy of you hypocrites, as it is written: 'This people honor Me with their lips, but their heart is far from Me,*
> *⁷ And in vain they worship Me, teaching as doctrines the commandments of men.'*
> *⁸ For laying aside the commandment of God, you hold the tradition of men, the washing of pitchers and cups, and many other such things you do.*
> *⁹ And He said to them, 'All too well you reject the commandment of God, that you may keep your tradition.'*
> *¹³ Making the word of God of no effect through your tradition which you have handed down. And many such things you do."*

How surprised the moneychangers were when Jesus began disrupting their corrupt practices. Jesus was going to cleanse His Father's house, and in doing so made a prophetic statement about His true temple, mankind. Through His redemptive work Jesus would make complete those who believe in Him.

> *Colossians 2:10*
> *"¹⁰ and you are complete in Him, who is the head of all principality and power."*

> *John 1:4-5*
> *"⁴ In Him was life, and the life was the light of men.*
> *⁵ And the light shines in the darkness, and the darkness did not apprehend it."*

A New Kind of Creation

I have already spoken about the uniqueness of man. God's command to multiply and fill the Earth is the same as Jesus commanding us to go into all the Earth and preach the gospel. But this time the Temple (man) will be much different.

When Jesus cleaned out the corruption in the Temple, He made a declaration that a new and better way was coming. No longer would the blood of bulls, goats and the ashes of red heifers be required. These were only a covering for sin for one year and could never be sufficient to make us truly clean. The sacrifice of lambs had to be repeated yearly with the constant reminder that sin reigns. In many ways this produces a chain of hopelessness around our spirit. The word of the Lord prophesied through Jeremiah states this.

> *Jeremiah 31:33-34*
> *³³ "But this is the covenant that I will make with the house of Israel after those days, says the LORD: I will put My law in their minds, and write it on their hearts; and I will be their God, and they shall be My people.*
> *³⁴ No more shall every man teach his neighbor, and every man his brother, saying, 'Know the LORD,' for they all shall know Me, from the least of them to the greatest of them, says the LORD.* ***For I will forgive their iniquity, and their sin I will remember no more.****"* (emphasis mine)

The sacrifice of Jesus and His blood was not a sacrifice to just cover sins but to totally remove them, even the stain of its corruption. Hebrews 1:3. This cannot be understood by the natural mind. Jesus is bringing us to the place where we can be "born of His Spirit" which is a supernatural work only the Holy Spirit can do. The actions Jesus took that day were not a last-minute purging of a structure. He was demonstrating that his last and final act of going to the cross would be violent but was necessary for the complete removal of the old system of sacrifices. He would soon be instituting a New Covenant and a new and living way to approach the Lord Most High.

When the Lord says a new creation, He is not talking about a "remodel" but a creation that has never existed before. Even the angels had no idea what was about to be changed in the heart of every man and woman who would be "reborn" by the Spirit of God. This would be much better than the original creation of mankind.

> *Hebrews 8:6*
> *"6 But now He has obtained a more excellent ministry, inasmuch as He is also Mediator of a better covenant, which was established on better promises."*

If the angels were astonished at the nature of man at creation, how much more would they marvel at the regeneration of the human spirit at salvation? Could they be asking, "What is it, or how can this be?" The Bible tells us that angels are ministering spirits sent to help those who are heirs of salvation. As they help us on our journey, do they ever go to the Lord and say, "This one has a glitch. You need to do something." I know my angel must have worn out running shoes and perhaps a few lost feathers. Salvation is a mystery to the Heavenly Hosts.

The Way is Open

When we stop to think of all Jesus did prior to His crucifixion and how completely He was in control, His actions at the Temple and with the fig tree are truly amazing. Jesus knows the depth of hatred the devil has for God and His creation. Our adversary's immense pride has consumed him and deceived him into thinking he can outwit God. Satan truly thinks he is now in control of God's greatest creation. He does not realize that it is God who has set the adversary up to destroy himself. God did this by working through the one, perfect man (Jesus) to open the way to the Father through the greatest sacrifice of all, the Lamb of God.

At the death and resurrection of Jesus Christ the Father demonstrated His acceptance of Jesus' sacrificed blood as full payment for our sins when He tore in two the Veil between the Holy Place and the Holy of Holies. This further demonstrated that a new and living way is now open into the very presence of God to anyone who would come.

Satan thought he could remove the Son of God by killing Him. Instead, Jesus' actions were instrumental in doing these four things:

> 1) satisfying the Father's justice and wiping out the handwriting of requirements written against us.
> 2) bringing into existence a new creation which was God's plan all along.
> 3) providing an open door into the throne room of God.
> 4) equipping this new creation with the power and authority of Heaven to continually move against Satan's kingdom.

Three days after the crucifixion was a really, really bad day for the devil. Praise God! The shout of life still reverberates. O death, where is your sting? O grave, where is your victory? JESUS IS ALIVE!!!

1 Corinthians 2:7-10
"⁷ But we speak the wisdom of God in a mystery, the hidden wisdom which God ordained before the ages for our glory,
⁸ which none of the rulers of this age knew; for had they known; they would not have crucified the Lord of glory.
⁹ But as it is written: "Eye has not seen, nor ear heard, nor have entered into the heart of man the things which God has prepared for those who love Him.
¹⁰ But God has revealed them to us through His Spirit. For the Spirit searches all things, yes, the deep things of God." (emphasis mine)

Hebrews 9:26
"But now, once at the end of the ages, He has appeared to put away sin by the sacrifice of Himself."

2 Corinthians 5:21
"²¹ For He made Him who knew no sin to be sin for us, that we might become the righteousness of God in Him."

Even in our fallen condition, lost and living in sin as children of darkness, God still sees us as having great value. Jesus wants to cleanse you just as He did the Temple in Jerusalem. Kingdom life is not a spectator sport existence. It is a life of transformation and power.

Cleansing Brings Healing

Our Lord and Father knows there is much work to be done in our heart in order to get His life and light flowing through us. He does not draw back, and neither should we. We have just started this journey, and many destiny moments lie ahead of us. There is much to be learned and revealed. As we fellowship with Him in worship and read His Word, His strength becomes our strength. Jesus then receives the reward of His suffering which is His life flowing out of us to others.

Once Jesus cleansed the Court of the Gentiles from the moneychangers, the sick, the lame and the blind were able to come in. And as they came, Jesus healed them. This is the same picture we see in Psalm 105:37 that says not one feeble was among them. Since at rebirth we become the Temple of God, Jesus can heal our feebleness. We are no longer spiritually blind or lame. It is time to move forward in faith and live, knowing we are equipped with the authority to minister the Kingdom of God to those who are lost, sick and in bondage.

Before Christ and After Christ

The Cross of Jesus Christ now stands as a citadel in the crossroads of history. From this point forward in history everything changed for humanity. Every other nation thereafter would see Jesus as the central figure in history. Our very calendars are a testament to this. Everything in history is seen as before Jesus Christ, B.C. (literally, Before Christ), and everything after Jesus Christ is A.D. which is Latin for "The Year of our Lord." At salvation after you are born again you, too, will view your life as "before Christ" and "after Christ" for you have been eternally changed by the Spirit of the Living God.

Jesus fulfilled the directive of His Father to the last detail. Every requirement of the Law was fulfilled in Christ. There was nothing left undone. Now, all that is required of us is to repent, turn from sin to Him, and enter into His finished work by faith. As we learn to trust Him in our obedience to His Holy Spirit and His written Word, we can live in our destiny and divine purpose. The penalty for sin has been paid in full. Our lives can now reflect His glory.

> *Mark 16:17-18*
> *"17 And these signs will follow those who believe: In My name they will cast out demons; they will speak with new tongues;*
> *18 they will take up serpents; and if they drink anything deadly, it will by no means hurt them; they will lay hands on the sick, and they will recover."*

Learning to Live as God's Chosen People

Jesus wants to flow out of us to a lost world held in darkness. He wants us to function as His Temple and become instruments of righteousness. Only you can do what God has planned for you, not your pastor or spouse or anyone else, only you. He places the light of His presence in you. He wants you fired up with the fire of the Holy Spirit to pull down strongholds and to be, not just a conqueror, but more than a conqueror.

> *Romans 8:37*
> *In all these things we are **more than conquerors** through Him who loved us.* (emphasis mine)

We speak much of the Holy Spirit coming as a dove. However, He only came as a dove upon Jesus who was sinless and perfect. Every other time the Holy Spirit was present, as on the Day of Pentecost and afterwards, He came as a purging fire upon them. This was prophesied by John the Baptist in Luke 3:16 when he said Jesus would baptize with the Holy Spirit and fire. The Holy Spirit comes as a purging fire upon those who are seeking the Kingdom of God's righteousness. We desperately need the holy refining fire of the altar of the Most High God. Our Lord wants us to have hearing ears. He is equipping us for our journey, tuning our ears to hear His voice, and giving clear direction on how to live in Him.

Philippians 2:13
"¹³ For it is God who works in you both to will and to do for His good pleasure."

Isaiah 56:7
"⁷ Even them I will bring to my Holy mountain, and make them joyful in My house of prayer. Their burnt offerings and their sacrifices will be accepted on my altar; for My house shall be called a house of prayer for all nations."

2 Peter 1:2-4
"² Grace be multiplied to you in the knowledge of God and of Jesus our Lord,
³ As His divine power has given to us all things that pertain to life and godliness, through the knowledge of Him who called us by glory and virtue,
⁴ By which have been given to us exceedingly great and precious promises, that through these you may be

partakers of His divine nature, having escaped the corruption that is in the world through lust."

Romans 16:20
"And the God of peace will crush Satan under your feet shortly. The grace of our God be with you."

Is It Really True?

Many Christians struggle with their past and wonder if they are truly saved. The voice of the liar keeps speaking and trying to cause doubt and unbelief. He uses words in the same way as he did in the garden hoping we will fall for the same deception. He wants to cause us to doubt God's Word, His love, and His faithfulness. Remember what Jesus said in John 8:44? The devil is a murderer and a liar and is, in fact, the father of all lies. If the liar can get us to fall to his temptation, he will steal, kill, and destroy everything good and wholesome in our lives.

This is a very real and often a never-ending battle for many. I am going to list several verses to encourage you. These scripture verses have ministered to me. I hope you will find encouragement in them also.

Numbers 23:19
"God is not a man, that He should lie, nor a son of man, that He should repent. Has He said, and will He not do? Or has He spoken, and will He not make it good?"

Titus 1:2
"In hope of eternal life which God, who cannot lie, promised before time began."

Psalm 103:12
"As far as the east is from the west, so far has He removed our transgressions from us."

Isaiah 43:25
"I, even I, am He who blots out your transgressions for My own sake; And I will not remember your sins."

When we are born again, the Lord God takes His rightful place in our lives. He moves in completely. Nothing of Himself is left out. Remember, He is LIFE and LIGHT. Think of this. In your **spirit** you are full of pure light, and there is not one shadow or dark area within you, because there is no darkness in Him. You are a New Creation. The old has passed away, and all has become new. You are now the righteousness of God in Christ Jesus. The Lord is present with all of His kingdom glory and power.

Ephesians 5:8
"For you were once darkness, but now you are light in the Lord. Walk as children of light."

Just being clean is not the end of the matter. It is just the beginning of our journey to becoming more than a conqueror. Along this journey we will face things from our past that need to be dealt with, and Jesus is going to begin that instruction on day two when He curses the fig tree.

This is a journey of faith and trust. You must remember that the adversary will try to gain access through your eye and ear gates so he can gain control of your head (imagination) to nail or hook you to chaos. He is cunning and subtle. Be on guard.

Chapter Eight

Cursing the Fig Tree

We may view the cleansing of the Temple as a separate event and not related to the fig tree moment, but they are very much intertwined. In many ways they mirror the deliverance of Israel from Egypt. Their journey through the wilderness was designed to prepare them for their destination and inheritance which God had promised to them. Scripture tells us their deliverance and journey were recorded as examples for us on how to respond or not to respond in our own destiny moments. We all encounter similar challenges and fears along the journey through life. Will we respond in faith believing or in doubt and fear? How we do respond will be made evident by the words we speak, and the words we speak will produce an action, and these together produce life or death. The choice is ours.

The cursing of the fig tree is not just another event leading up to the crucifixion but a moment of revelation in confronting the kingdom of darkness. The morning after Jesus cleansed the Temple, He and the disciples returned to Jerusalem.

> Matthew 21:18-19
> *"¹⁸Now in the morning, as He returned to the city, He was hungry.*
> *¹⁹And seeing a fig tree by the road, He came to it and found nothing on it but leaves, and said to it, 'Let no fruit grow on you ever again.' Immediately the fig tree withered away."*

Jesus was NOT unleashing a fleshly anger at the tree because He was hungry. The fig tree goes all the way back to the Garden of Eden where Adam and Eve clothed themselves with fig leaves trying to cover their sin.

Not all fig trees are fruitless, nor are all the mountains they grow from bad ground. Jesus was looking for fruit. If fruit had been there, the tree would have remained. The scripture is clear that we are the planting of the Lord planted in the courts of our God, and we will be fresh and flourishing bringing forth fruitful abundance. Psalm 92:12-15; John 15:16.

Jesus is confronting everything involved with the fig tree and its lack of fruit. How did it get into this condition? Why was there no fruit on it? We have this same event recorded in Mark 11:12-13 which states it was not the time or season for figs. This can be confusing. Why would Jesus curse a tree that was not in season? Here is an interesting fact about fig trees.

The *International Standard Bible Encyclopedia* gives us insight into this verse.

> *"When the young leaves are newly appearing, in April, every fig tree which is going to bear fruit at all will have some **"taksh"** **(immature figs)** upon it, even though*

> *"the time of figs", i.e. of ordinary edible figs-either early or late crop, was not yet. This taksh is not only eaten today, but it is **sure evidence**, even when it falls, that the tree bearing it is not barren."*
> (emphasis mine)

Simple put. If a fig tree does not have these early immature figs, it will not bear any fruit later. It is a barren tree and needs to be removed.

Jesus made a prophetic declaration when he cleansed the Temple and cursed the fig tree. All who believe and are born of the Spirit of God are destined to become a holy habitation full of light and power. They will be more than conquerors, pulling down strongholds of darkness and advancing the Kingdom of God. Those who are born again may not see themselves as an overcomer, but God does. Newly born Christians are babes in Christ, but they can grow and mature in Christ as they daily walk with Him. Romans 4:17 references Abraham on this.

> *Romans 4:17*
> *"^{17} As it is written, 'I have made you a father of many nations, in the presence of Him whom he believed—God, who gives life to the dead and calls those things which do not exist as though they did'."*

This is the prophetic nature of the cleansing of the Temple and the cursing of the fig tree. God sees us complete because of the powerful blood of Jesus. Yet, there is a shaking that often takes place in those areas of our lives where we are not yet aligned with God's purpose.

> Hebrews 12:24-29
> "²⁴ *To Jesus the Mediator of the New Covenant, and to the blood of sprinkling that speaks better things than that of Abel.*
> ²⁵ *See that you do not refuse Him who speaks. For if they did not escape who refused Him who spoke on Earth, much more shall we not escape if we turn away from Him who speaks from heaven,*
> ²⁶ *Whose voice then shook the Earth; but now He has promised, saying, "Yet once more I shake not only the Earth, but also heaven."*
> ²⁷ *Now this, "Yet once more," indicates* **the removal of those things that are being shaken,** *as of things that are made, that the things which cannot be shaken may remain.* (emphasis mine)
> ²⁸ *Therefore, since we are receiving a kingdom which cannot be shaken, let us have grace, by which we may serve God acceptably with reverence and godly fear.*
> ²⁹ *For our God is a consuming fire."*

The phrase "the removal of those things that are being shaken" is at the heart of the fig tree event. Some things in our lives need to die in order for the life of Christ to live through us.

> Galatians 2:10
> "*I am crucified with Christ, nevertheless I live. Yet not I, but Christ lives within me.*"

Because of the fall in the Garden of Eden our response to any wrong doing is to endeavor to "cover" our sin. We do not realize the adversary is trying to build a stronghold in that area of our lives again. We begin to live a "fig-leaf" life by trying to work our way back into favor with the Lord. Just as Adam and Eve used fig leaves in an attempt to hide their shame, we too can be drawn back into that trap. We may even hide behind religious fig leaves among those around us.

The only fruit this tree can produce is the fruit of excuses, false humility, and blame. We may even liken the fig tree to doctrines of demons which twist the Word of God into a new type of gospel. Many today are deceived and do this, but we are not fooling God. Compromises can keep us from fulfilling God's divine plan for our lives, thus eliminating us as a threat to Satan's kingdom. Jesus is taking this opportunity to instruct His disciples.

The Lord sees it all. What we see as condemnation, the Holy Spirit sees as a fruitless fig tree, and He brings conviction. Repentance and confession from the heart is what the Lord desires. This is how you deal with fruitless areas of your life. This is how you overcome your adversary.

How often do we hear someone say they hope their good works outweigh their bad? In fact, every world religion operates on a work-based system to appease their god in the hope of a blessed eternity. Some even have the idea they will have many lifetimes to get it right and say, "I just hope in my next life, I'm not a roach or something worse." There is also the snare of "penitence" that has enslaved so many, giving a false hope that this is what God demands to get back into favor with Him. These are all fig leaves and will give a false sense of security, thereby causing more burdens and producing more barrenness. People may despair that the joy of the Lord seems to be only for certain ones or is an unattainable myth. Either way, life for them is only a living death. Deep down they know something is not right. Deep down they hope there is something better.

A New Covenant, A New Life

The sacrifice that was performed by God in the garden and later fully established at Mt. Sinai were only temporary coverings until the coming of the promised Seed. They only covered sin temporarily and had to be repeated yearly with the constant reminder we are sinners. Hebrews chapter 10 makes clear that all other forms of sacrifice and worship previously established were being completely done away with by Christ's "once and for all sacrifice" of Himself. No amount of animal blood could do what Jesus accomplished by dying on the cross in obedience to His Father's will.

> Hebrews 8:6-7
> "⁶ But now He has obtained a more excellent ministry, inasmuch as He is also Mediator of a better covenant, which was established on better promises.
> ⁷ For if that first covenant had been faultless, then no place would have been sought for a second."

Jesus is declaring to the world. You will never be good enough, nor can you work hard enough to gain eternal salvation. **Only what I have done** will bring you to salvation and your divine purpose. We can only enter into Jesus by His shed blood. We must remain in fellowship with Him for our lives to produce what the Father has ordained for us. We are only complete in Him.

Learning to Walk in God's Ways

Being born again is an instant work of the Holy Spirit. But learning to walk and live in Kingdom Life and the power of the resurrection is a daily process. Spiritual, fruitless fig trees have their roots in the kingdom of darkness. Not one of us chose to be born into sin. That decision was made for us in the Garden of Eden. Sin and death were passed down to us as our inheritance, and through the process of time you and I were born into this world.

In many things about life you had no control. But God knew the details of how, where and when you would be born. He knew you before creation and wrote of you in detail. God saw you in your mother's womb, and His thoughts of you outnumber the sand. How marvelous is that?

> *Psalm 139:13-18*
> *"*^{13} *For You formed my inward parts; You covered me in my mother's womb.*
> ^{14} *I will praise You, for I am fearfully and wonderfully made; Marvelous are Your works, and that my soul knows very well.*
> ^{15} *My frame was not hidden from You, When I was made in secret, and skillfully wrought in the lowest parts of the Earth.*
> ^{16} *Your eyes saw my substance, being yet unformed. And in Your book, they all were written; The days fashioned for me; When as yet there were none of them.*
> ^{17} *How precious also are Your thoughts to me, O God! How great is the sum of them!*
> ^{18} *If I should count them, they would be more in number than the sand; When I awake, I am still with You."*

No matter the circumstances of your birth you were given these wonderful gifts: faith, hope, and the power of choice. As we navigate our time on Earth, the kingdom we live in will be evident to those around us, especially to the unseen powers. Just as Israel was delivered from Egypt, we too can be delivered from our sin at the point of salvation. Just as their minds and imaginations were still in bondage, we too can have thought patterns shaped by our former bondage. The destiny moments of our daily journey will reveal many destructive imaginations. Our Heavenly Father wants us to confront them and conquer them, and He wants to see deliverance brought to ourselves and those around us.

It is God's right to expect us to live as sons and daughters of the Most High as He has given us everything that pertains to life and godliness.

Our Baggage

Old nasty baggage. We all have it. Where does it come from, and how do we rid ourselves of it? Many things that affect our lives, whether good or bad, mold us into the individuals we are. The things we see, hear and learn give direction to our lives. For the most part we may have had good examples set before us, and we have learned many valuable things for living a happy, productive life. Yet, it is also true that we can bare the mark of destructive tendencies and mindsets. We will continue in these unless we uproot them. The fruit of the past, some good and some bad, will continue to be produced. We should cultivate the good fruit but deal with the bad fruit in God's way.

The entrance to these thought patterns and attitudes came by way of our eyes and ears. This is evident by the way the adversary tempted Eve. He convinced her that she was being denied something. Once his words were planted, they quickly took root, and she was taken captive by desire. She then gave to Adam, and the flood gates of death and destruction came bursting forth. Adam listened. He saw, and his own desire lead him to partake of the fruit as well. The Bible indicates that Adam was not deceived. He knew exactly what was at stake.

Words are Seeds

Jesus tells us in Mark 4:14 and in Luke 8:11 that words are seed and once planted they will produce a harvest. A seed always produces a tree after its kind. In Genesis 3:15 God judged Satan and declared there would be enmity (hostility) between the seed of the adversary and the Seed of the woman. The Seed of the woman in Genesis 3:15 is speaking of the coming of Jesus Christ. Here at the beginning in the Garden of Eden we see the onset of the battle between two kingdoms. Sin, death and destruction will reign only for a season.

What we also see here is that the battle of the two kingdoms began with words, <u>just four words</u> that caused Eve to question God. **"Has God indeed said?"** Genesis 3:1. God created everything with the power of His spoken word. Hebrews 1:3 declares that creation is held together by God's spoken word. All throughout scripture we are told to be careful about what comes out of our mouths. Our words have the power to establish a narrative, whether true or false. All we have to do is listen to the media outlets to realize this powerful truth.

> *Matthew 12:36*
> *"*[36] *But I say to you that for every idle word, men may speak, they will give account of it in the day of judgment."*

Jesus is not trying to bring fear but to emphasize the power we all have with our own words. We hear words, and we immediately form a picture in our minds of what is being told to us. We reinforce those words by repeating them over and over again, and we underestimate the power they have upon us and how they shape our identity. Words are seed and will produce a harvest in our lives and in the lives of those around us. What you agree with and speak about becomes your identity.

A Cunning Attack

Do you recall how the adversary approached Eve? It was in a **cunning** manner. The Hebrew letters for the word cunning gave us an overview of the attack. <u>The eye was the target in order to gain control of the head, so he could nail or hook them to chaos</u>. (Refer back to the chapter on God's Mandate) Do you see how powerful words can be? This action is what the adversary still uses in the destruction of mankind today. We are able to sum this up in Eve's response to the attack of the liar.

> *Genesis 3:6*
> *"So, when the woman saw that the tree was good for food, that it was pleasant to the eyes, and a tree desirable to make one wise, she took of its fruit and ate. She also gave to her husband with her, and he ate."*

> *1 John 2:16*
> *"For all that is in the world—the lust of the flesh, the lust of the eyes, and the pride of life - is not of the Father but is of the world."*

As a whole, humanity is completely blind to the power God gave us at creation. He gave us the power of speech and the power of choice. Even after the fall in the garden God did not remove these. We still have a choice in our lives on how we will live and what we will say. Changing how we think and speak is a choice we can make if we are willing to do so.

God offers redemption to those who believe and surrender their lives to Him. Those who come to Him can live a life full of purpose and freedom from the bondage of sin. We can now choose to use our voice to share the gospel and bring deliverance to a lost world. The following is a sampling of scriptures that deal with the tongue, our eyes and our ears.

Proverbs 18:21
"²¹ Death and life are in the power of the tongue,
And those who love it will eat its fruit."

Galatians 6:7
"⁷ Do not be deceived, God is not mocked; for whatever a man sows, that he will also reap."

In these two verses alone, we see the words we speak will bring either death or life. When words of doubt, fear and unbelief are sown then doubt, fear and unbelief will be harvested. When words of faith, trust and hope are sown then faith, hope and trust will be harvested. And the harvested words will always produce more than what was sown.

Mark 4:8-9
"⁸ But other seed fell on good ground and yielded a crop that sprang up, increased and produced: some thirtyfold, some sixty, and some a hundred."

⁹ And He said to them, "He who has ears to hear, let him hear!"

Luke 8:8
"⁸ But others fell on good ground, sprang up, and yielded a crop a hundredfold." When He had said these things He cried, 'He who has ears to hear, let him hear'!"

Be Careful What and How You Hear

Jesus is talking about the Word of God being spoken and how it takes root and produces a harvest. The adversary does the same thing with words. Whether spoken or heard, all words are like seed. With this admonition let us look at how Jesus instructs us to <u>guard</u> both the things we <u>hear</u> and <u>see</u>.

Mark uses the phrase, "Take heed **what** you hear."

Mark 4:24
Then He said to them, "Take heed <u>what</u> you hear. With the same measure you use, it will be measured to you; and to you who hear, more will be given."

Luke uses the phrase, "Take heed **how** you hear."

Luke 8:18
Therefore, take heed <u>how</u> you hear. For whoever has, to him more will be given; and whoever does not have, even what he seems to have will be taken from him."

The phrase "take heed" is of great importance.

Strong's Concordance # 991 - to look at (literally or figuratively), behold, beware, lie, look (on, to), perceive, regard, see, sight, take heed.

Just in the phrase "take heed" we see an indication of **sight** in both what we see and what we hear. When we hear something, a picture is formed in our minds like what happens when we read a book. This is how our imagination works. We may not always have a choice on what we hear, but how we assimilate those words are in our control. We give them authority to shape our life, or we rebuke them. They will build us up or tear us down.

Both writers emphasize the importance of "guarding" our lives. Just as Adam was instructed to guard the garden, we also have the same mandate. We are the planting of the Lord destined to bring forth a harvest.

We have all heard the phrase, "Sticks and stones may break my bones, but words will never harm me." That saying is one of the biggest lies the adversary has ever planted in our vernacular. Words are the very foundation upon which we form our ideas and responses to life. Mark uses the word "what," and Luke uses the word "how." Jesus is stressing the importance of what and how we process the things we hear and see.

In Exodus chapters 13 and 14 when the twelve spies returned, ten of the spies said they were not able to take the land because of the giants and strongly fortified cities. Their words were about their own ability to conquer the land. God never told them to conquer the land in their own ability. Joshua and Caleb were the only two spies who believed God. They did not deny there were giants or strongly fortified cities. This is important. We are never told to deny the problem. Joshua and Caleb viewed God as a promise keeper and greater than their enemies. We should do the same. Satan wants to preempt and abort the promises of God with fear and doubts about God's goodness.

The majority of the people agreed with the negative report of the ten spies and began to fortify the words they heard in their own hearts and minds. Not only did the majority fail to receive the promise, but they called God a liar and accused Him of wanting them to die in the wilderness. They were partly correct in saying God wanted them to die. God wanted them to die to the ways of Egypt that had enslaved both their bodies and minds for far too long.

God wanted them to rule and reign as His people. The Israelites were to subdue the Earth as Adam had been instructed but had failed to do so. They needed their minds renewed to think and act like God intended. The apostle Paul instructs us in Romans 12:1 that we likewise need to be transformed by the renewing of our minds. Possessing your inheritance is not possible with a slave mentality. Transformation is required.

This helps us to understand what Jesus meant in Mark 4:24-25 and Luke 8:18. We need to guard what we hear, but we also need to guard how we process the things we do hear. What we hear and how we process those words will either strengthen or weaken our lives in the journey to our destination and inheritance.

Your Choice to Make

We live in an instant information world full of distractions. We desperately need to be guarding **what** we hear. This is not always possible. However, there are times when we do have a choice in this. Examples are: gossip, the type of music we listen to, movies we watch, programs that stir carnal thoughts, and so forth. This may sound legalistic, but we have to be honest with ourselves. Do these things strengthen me in the Lord or weaken me? Here again is an opportunity to grow stronger in the Lord or strengthen the bondages in our lives.

> *Psalm 19:14*
> *"Let the words of my mouth and the meditation of my heart be acceptable in Your sight, O LORD, my strength and my Redeemer."*
>
> *Psalm 119:37*
> *"37 Turn away my eyes from looking at worthless things, and revive me in Your way."*

The psalmist is actively seeking the help and wisdom of the Lord in order not to grieve Him. We have been instructed not to grieve the Holy Spirit. It is to our advantage to respond quickly to His voice even if in our natural mind it does not make sense. The Lord desires that we mature and come into the full potential He has created us to be. Now that we are His children, the only thing He desires to die in us are the plantings of the old man, and that is a process called sanctification. This sanctification process is a daily relational walk with the Lord and is an essential part of our new life. We will not always get it right. He knows this, but we can keep our eyes on Him and cultivate hearing ears.

When a fig tree moment or a stronghold is made evident in your life, that is the appointed time to remove it. The process of removal will begin with the confession of your mouth that you need it removed. The first step to deliverance is always admitting there is a stronghold in your life. Then a renouncing of its hold and power over you is required. We are to actively disown that tree or stronghold and bring it to the Cross of Christ for it to die.

> 2 Corinthians 4:2
> *"² But we have renounced the hidden things of shame, not walking in craftiness nor handling the word of God deceitfully, but by manifestation of the truth commending ourselves to every man's conscience in the sight of God."*

The word "renounce" in *Strong's Concordance #550* means *"to say '<u>off</u>' for oneself, i.e. disown — renounce."*

> 2 Corinthians 10:3-6
> *"³ For though we walk in the flesh, we do not war according to the flesh.*
> *⁴ For the weapons of our warfare are not carnal but mighty in God for pulling down strongholds,*
> *⁵ casting down arguments and every high thing that exalts itself against the knowledge of God, bringing every thought into captivity to the obedience of Christ,*
> *⁶ and being ready to punish all disobedience when your obedience is fulfilled."*

In this spiritual conflict, only spiritual weapons are effective. I refer back to Matthew 17:17-21 where a father brought his demon possessed son to the disciples to be delivered. The disciples were unable to heal the boy, and Jesus publicly rebuked them.

> *Matthew 17:17*
> *"Then Jesus answered and said, 'O faithless and perverse generation, how long shall I be with you? How long shall I bear with you? Bring him here to Me'."*

Jesus was nearing the end of His time with the disciples. These were the men He would empower to reach a lost world, and they needed to pay close attention to Him. Jesus knew what was about to happen in just a few days. They did not. He saw the bigger picture. He saw their weaknesses and desired for them to rise to the occasion. Their world is about to be turned upside down.

> *Matthew 17:20-21*
> *"[20] So Jesus said to them, "Because of your unbelief; for assuredly, I say to you, if you have faith as a mustard seed, you will say to this mountain, 'Move from here to there,' and it will move; and nothing will be impossible for you.*
> *[21] However, this kind does not go out except by prayer and fasting."*

Bring the Flesh Under Submission

The spiritual realm does not respond to the rebuke of the physical realm. It only responds to the living spirit of someone who is born again and has a thriving relationship with the Lord. Bringing our flesh under submission to the Holy Spirit is not always an easy task. Our flesh has been conditioned to its comfort zone, and if we are truthful, our flesh is in more control than we want to admit.

Not only do we have fruitless fig trees and strongholds deposited by outside sources, but we have been busy planting trees and building strongholds ourselves. The instruction was given to fast and pray. We often think of fasting as doing without food, and that is the most common form of fasting. When we do fast from food, it does not take long for us to realize how much we love it. But you may also fast from something other than food, and that is between you and the Lord. Fasting for spiritual reasons should involve praying as well, otherwise, you are only dieting. The spiritual warfare we enter into at this time can become intense. Our adversary knows the power and strength that is released when our spirit is locked away in the secret place with the Lord.

Fasting not only strengthens the spiritual senses, but it will also drive out unbelief. When Jesus said this kind only comes out by prayer and fasting, He was saying that we will gain victory, not only over demons, but also over the weakness of unbelief in our own spirit and mind.

2 Corinthians 10:5
"5 Casting down arguments and every high thing that exalts itself against the knowledge of God, bringing every thought into captivity to the obedience of Christ."

The weapons God has given will do what He said they would do - pull down the high places and uproot everything that exalts itself above God. These things are demonic in nature and have their roots in the original rebellion.

Isaiah 14:12-15
"12 How you are fallen from heaven, O Lucifer, son of the morning! How you are cut down to the ground, You who weakened the nations!

¹³ *For you have said in your heart: 'I will ascend into heaven; I will exalt my throne above the stars of God; I will also sit on the mount of the congregation on the farthest sides of the north;*
¹⁴ *I will ascend above the heights of the clouds; I will be like the Most High.'*
¹⁵ *Yet you shall be brought down to Sheol, to the lowest depths of the Pit."*

Grace to Live Victoriously

The adversary has used mankind's fallen nature to set up his throne in the hearts of every man and woman, and he has brought unimaginable sorrow and suffering into the world. All of our lives bare the fruit of rebellion against God and His authority. After we are born of His Spirit, our lives will be a divine paradox in many ways. The life we have now should be evident to all, and yet we may find ourselves manifesting two kingdoms and wondering why this is so. This is when we find that the same grace by which we were saved, now becomes our instructor to teach us how to live victoriously in God's Kingdom. This is the marvelous power of God's grace.

> *Titus 2:11-15* (emphasis mine)
> *"¹¹ For the **grace of God that brings salvation** has appeared to all men,*
> *¹² **teaching us** that, denying ungodliness and worldly lusts, we should live soberly, righteously, and godly in the present age,*
> *¹³ looking for the blessed hope and glorious appearing of our great God and Savior Jesus Christ.*

> ¹⁴ *who gave Himself for us, that He might redeem us from every lawless deed and purify for Himself His own special people, zealous for good works.*
> ¹⁵ *Speak these things, exhort, and rebuke with all authority. Let no one despise you."*

When the Lord moves in, He will begin the pruning process. His light and glory now fully inhabit us, and He begins to illuminate our mind and spirit. As we allow His light to shine into our hearts, we should expect Him to expose our hidden areas that have not been fully surrendered to Him. This is not to condemn but to strength us for our journey and to help us make wise choices in our daily destiny moments.

The only way for deliverance is obedience to the Word of God. The Lord could very easily remove our fig trees without our participation, but we still have a choice in these matters. Our freedom of choice is still intact. We can resist or walk in obedience to His Word. He has chosen to call us into the spiritual fight to manifest the power of His blood and His glorious resurrection. We were created to rule and reign with Him. Ruling and reigning are part of being "More than a Conqueror."

On your journey the Lord will lead you to the fruitless fig trees in your life where your active participation is required for the removal of strongholds. These strongholds must be dealt with before moving on. There are spiritual truths to be learned at each fig tree. God's wisdom is readily available. All you need to do is ask.

Warring in the spirit with prayer, praise, and worship and putting on the armor of God is not just a mental or verbal exercise. It is a daily reminder of who Jesus is in our lives. He is our protection. He is our dwelling place and covering.

Without Him we are powerless, but through Him we can do all things.

Chapter Nine

Facing the Mountain

The Fig Tree's Source of Power. When the disciples saw the fig tree, they asked how it withered so soon. At this question Jesus informed them that they had the ability to do the same thing and even more. They too could speak to the mountain, and it will be removed from their midst for they had been given the faith to do so. They did not understand it then, but everything they had witnessed Jesus do up to this point were "destiny moments" given to them for their learning. They did not realize they were in the School of the Spirit. They were interacting in events the prophets had prophesied about and desired to see. Each disciple would have more destiny moments ahead of them each designed to strengthen their faith, so they could face their adversary and see him flee.

Mountains are mentioned 137 times in the scripture. They were used as points of reference as well as places of worship. We may be familiar with Mount Zion, God's holy mountain, and Mount Sinai where Moses met with God to receive the Law. There are also the mountains of Moriah where Abraham was instructed to offer Isaac and Mount Carmel where the prophet, Elijah, encountered the prophets of Baal and defeated them.

In the New Testament we see Jesus transfigured on Mount Hermon and praying on the Mount of Olives. He was crucified on Mount Calvary, and His future return will be to the Mount of Olives. When Jesus cursed the fig tree, the disciples marveled that it could wither so quickly. Jesus responded by telling them that if they believed, they could do the same and even remove the mountain.

> *Matthew 21:21-22*
> *"21So, Jesus answered and said to them, 'Assuredly, I say to you, if you have faith and do not doubt, you will not only do what was done to the fig tree, but also if you say to this mountain, 'Be removed and be cast into the sea,' it will be done.*
> *22And all things, whatever you ask in prayer, believing, you will receive'."*

Jesus indicates the fig tree has its roots in a mountain that needs to be removed. When Jesus instructed them to speak to the mountain, he was not referencing a physical mountain but a spiritual stronghold or high place which the adversary had established. Destructive strongholds can take hold because people have been part of Satan's kingdom at some point or have had his destructive words spoken over them. All of the fruitless fig trees established in our lives and all of our excuses have their roots in a mountain. The tree roots are fed from the ground from which it grows, so just removing the tree is not enough. The source of its growth must be removed. If not, the mountain will always be a reminder of our past. If it is not removed, it will be warring for our attention, and even a seedling of that tree that has withered could begin to take root again.

Throughout His ministry Jesus always referenced the physical world to illustrate the spiritual. Too often we are unaware of the spiritual world to which we are connected. We do not realize how much our adversary watches and listens and influences our speech or thoughts. He is ever looking for an opportunity to trip us up.

Just as we will face many fruitless fig trees in our lives that need to be removed, there will also be mountain strongholds. Being born and raised in a Christian environment does not exclude us from having our lives influenced by sin for all have sinned and fallen short of the glory of God. The fight we are engaged in requires the wisdom and guidance of heaven.

1 Peter 2:11
"Beloved, I beg you as sojourners and pilgrims, abstain from fleshly lusts which war against the soul."

The Mountain has a Name

As with the removal of the fruitless fig tree, there must be an acknowledgment of the presence and influence of the mountain. As we follow Jesus and are transformed by Him, His word and covering of righteousness gives us authority over the works of the devil. Never forget that your adversary is a thief who comes to kill, steal and destroy. John 10:10. The prophet, Jeremiah, gives us the actual name of the mountain we face.

Jeremiah 51:24-26 (emphasis mine)
*"²⁴ 'And I will repay Babylon and all the inhabitants of Chaldea, for all the evil they have done in Zion in **your sight**,' says the LORD.*
*²⁵ 'Behold, I am against **you**, O **destroying mountain, who** destroys all the Earth,' says the LORD. 'And I will stretch out My hand against **you**, roll **you** down from the rocks, and make **you** a burnt mountain.*
*²⁶ They shall not take from **you** a stone for a corner nor a stone for a foundation, but **you** shall be desolate forever,' says the LORD."*

Two mountains are mentioned here, Zion and the destroying mountain. I believe this is not only the Mountain of Zion but also the people of Zion, the original Temple and Jerusalem. The other is the destroying mountain that has held all of creation captive. When the Lord says, "I will do this in your sight," He means the destruction of the adversary will happen in Jerusalem at the crucifixion and resurrection of Jesus.

1 John 3:8
"He who sins is of the devil, for the devil has sinned from the beginning. For this purpose, the Son of God was manifested, that He might destroy the works of the devil."

The Lord indicates this mountain was and is a **created being** by referring to it as "you" and "who." Note the use of personal pronouns in the above-mentioned passage of scripture. This tells us that the mountain is not just a physical place but a place from which a spiritual entity can rule. This evil one only has one motive, and that is to bring as much destruction and chaos as he can to all the Earth and those who dwell in it. This is the description of the devil who entered the Garden of Eden and began his rule there. In Zechariah 4:6-7 Zerubbabel is instructed to speak to the mountain.

> *Zechariah 4:6-7* (emphasis mine)
> *⁶ So he answered and said to me: "This is the **word of the** LORD to Zerubbabel: 'Not by might nor by power, but by My Spirit,' says the LORD of hosts.*
> *⁷ 'Who are you, O great mountain? Before Zerubbabel you shall become a plain! And he shall bring forth the capstone with shouts of grace, grace to it'!"*

Zerubbabel is given very simple instructions. Speak the **Word** of the Lord with "shouts of grace, grace," and the mountain will become a plain.

Why shout "grace, grace?" Because it is only through God's redeeming grace that we have authority over the destroyer. In the beginning we were created to rule and reign under God's authority, but we gave our authority over to the devil and were transplanted into the kingdom of darkness where sin and death now rules. Only the light of the gospel and the blood of Jesus are able to redeem us and bring us back to our created purpose.

The Mountain Speaks

The instructions to the disciples regarding the mountain came immediately after Jesus cursed the fruitless fig tree. This journey requires an entering into Him. At the moment of our salvation we confessed our sin and need of His blood and grace. Our only participation in the work was repenting and turning from sin. It was the Holy Spirit who did the transforming work in us. As God's redeemed child free of the bondage of sin, we can begin to learn how to walk and talk like Him. A life of joy, peace, and purpose is now possible.

We are now in the School of the Spirit to transform us into instruments of righteousness. This instruction is needed to break free and leave behind the mental bondage of speaking and acting like slaves. As we learn how to live as the redeemed sons and daughters of the Living God, we become a living testimony to the transforming power of the cross.

The Israelites were freed from Egypt and faced many destiny moments on their journey to prepare them for their destination and inheritance. We will face many of our own fruitless fig trees and mountains in our journey. Each destiny moment is designed to reveal what needs to be cast off. What we choose in these moments will determine the quality of our Christian walk. We can even delay our arrival to our destination by resisting the Holy Spirit's work in us. This can leave us wondering through life for years in bondage to the effects of sin. Our choices will even determine if we will receive our promised inheritance here in this life. Don't misunderstand me. We are saved and going to Heaven when we accept Christ, but living victoriously over sin here on Earth is determined by our daily choices to follow in God's ways. You see, our inheritance is not just Heaven. God has an inheritance for you here on Earth. And that inheritance is found in Christ Jesus. Life is still a choice. Will we continue in our new-found faith or hold on to the old ways?

Hebrews 12:1
"Therefore, we also, since we are surrounded by so great a cloud of witnesses, let us lay aside every weight, and the sin which so easily ensnares us, and let us run with endurance the race that is set before us."

The strongman of the mountain we are up against will speak to us and endeavor to shame us. Through his lies he will try to convince us that we are not who God says we are in Jesus. He is scattering his seeds through false narratives, and he desires them to take root again in our life. Our posture is to resist him in the name of the Lord and the power of His shed blood. If you find this difficult, it is helpful to have people of like faith around in times of temptation, testing and despair. God is faithful. The way is open to His throne at any time to receive the help we need on our most difficult days.

Hebrews 4:16
"Let us therefore come boldly to the throne of grace, that we may obtain mercy and find grace to help in time of need."

Why is it Taking so Long?

God has brought us out of darkness by His amazing grace, and this grace is not a onetime event. It is an ever-present gift to teach and guide us. Titus 2:11-15. Growing in faith is a lifetime journey.

Our flesh still desires to control our spirit, and it will if we let it. Our struggles in life usually expose a weakness in us. This should not discourage us in any way. It is part of the journey of destiny moments, our choices. Will I enter into the flow of God's life or retreat back into old dead attitudes? To reach our full potential as a conqueror and even "more than a conqueror," we must relinquish control of our own will and yield to the Father's. It is the only way for His life and peace to be established in our lives.

We live in one of two kingdoms, the Kingdom of Light or the kingdom of darkness. Each kingdom will be manifested in the world by the actions of its citizens, and each kingdom operates within established boundaries or laws. There are no gray areas.

Matthew 6:24
"No one can serve two masters; for either he will hate the one and love the other, or else he will be loyal to the one and despise the other. You cannot serve God and mammon."

I have never heard a true, born again believer say, "Well, I am under grace, so it does not matter if I sin. Grace covers it all." This attitude is never present in the life of someone whose focus is truly on the Lord. It does not mean that we will never sin, but when we do, there is immediate conviction and repentance. We can be confident of this. The Holy Spirit will always reveal to us, at the very moment of temptation, if the choice I am about to make is pleasing to Him or not. Will I ask for help to overcome at that moment or disregard the warning? There have been times I chose poorly and suffered the consequences of my actions.

The same thing happened to Israel with their defeat at Ai in Joshua chapter 7. They relied on their own strength and wisdom and did not seek the Lord. As a result, they were soundly defeated. This goes back to the power we have to make choices.

Coming out of darkness does not remove the power of choice from us. We now have the strength to cast off the unprofitable works of darkness and bring forth fruits of righteousness. Our free-will remains intact. The choice is ours to make. God will not always intervene in every circumstance. When He does, it is by His grace alone. However, sometimes the Lord allows us to suffer the consequences of our poor choices to bring us the instruction and correction needed to redirect our steps back to Him. We will find He is always a merciful, loving Father welcoming us back to Himself.

Sadly, an attitude of compromise does exist in many which says any boundaries are legalism. Their excuse may be, "I was raised to believe this way of living is no big deal." I understand this is a growing process, and sanctification is a lifelong work of the Spirit of God within us. But there comes a time when our new life in Christ Jesus should begin to see the fruit of the Kingdom of God become more evident.

The only way to fail in our life with Christ is to quit and throw in the towel. If we are constantly looking back at what was, we will remain in bondage to a slave mentality. In this journey of choices, we are not powerless. The choice on where we set our gaze, our hopes and our dreams are solely ours and ours alone to make.

2 Corinthians 13:5
"5 Examine yourselves as to whether you are in the faith. Test yourselves. Do you not know yourselves, that Jesus Christ is in you? — unless indeed you are disqualified."

Keep your Gaze Fixed on Jesus

A person must look at where they are going, otherwise they will run into something or fall into a ditch. The direction of our gaze can become our greatest snare and can cause us to be entangled again in works of darkness. We often have a horizonal gaze, comparing ourselves with one another and building a mental scoreboard of the victories of others. When we do this, we seldom have victory or breakthrough. It becomes an open invitation for the adversary to plant seeds of bitterness against people, and a spirit of pride can enter in. When we are tempted to be upset with others, take those feelings to the Lord. Do not have a conversation with a snake. It will not end well.

Even bitterness against the Lord is possible if we do not have our prayers answered fast enough or in the way we think they should be. It takes a lot of spiritual maturity to patiently wait on the Lord and trust Him with the outcome.

I remember some years ago it was fashionable to get up every morning and quote Ephesians 6 and "put on the armor of God" piece by piece. I am not making light of that. It is an active exercise, and when done with understanding, it is a strength and blessing to you. But the problem we face is an incomplete understanding of Ephesians 5 and its instruction to us.

> *Ephesians 5:1-11*
> *"Therefore, be imitators of God as dear children.*
> *² And walk in love, as Christ also has loved us and given Himself for us, an offering and a sacrifice to God for a sweet-smelling aroma.*

> ³ *But fornication and all uncleanness or covetousness, let it not even be named among you, as is fitting for saints;*
> ⁴ *neither filthiness, nor foolish talking, nor coarse jesting, which are not fitting, but rather giving of thanks.*
> ⁵ *For this you know, that no fornicator, unclean person, nor covetous man, who is an idolater, has any inheritance in the kingdom of Christ and God.*
> ⁶ *Let no one deceive you with empty words, for because of these things the wrath of God comes upon the sons of disobedience.*
> ⁷ *Therefore do not be partakers with them*
> ⁸ *For you were once darkness, but now you are light in the Lord. Walk as children of light*
> ⁹ *for the fruit of the Spirit is in all goodness, righteousness, and truth,*
> ¹⁰ *finding out what is acceptable to the Lord.*
> ¹¹ *And have no fellowship with the unfruitful works of darkness, but rather expose them."*

God's holiness will not be associated with unrighteous lifestyles no matter how much the promises are quoted. This is tantamount to witchcraft and using the Word of God like a book of spells. This is an extremely dangerous place to live, as it opens one up to an unabated attack of the adversary to continue sowing seeds of destruction in our lives. Then, when the words we have quoted fail to bear the fruit we want, doubt and mistrust becomes the fruit brought forth.

Pastors and congregations who hold to the truth of scripture and who walk as the Holy Spirit directs will face attacks from those who resist the Truth. When a godly pastor or believer brings forth the Word of God under the anointing of the Holy Spirit, conviction grips the heart of the hearer. When a person feels this conviction from the Holy Spirit, one of two things are going to happen - repentance or rejection of the presented Truth of God's Word. If they reject the Truth, it may be displayed in anger against the speaker, and a possible confrontation may occur. When a person who desires to live righteously before the Lord is presented with the Truth of God's Word, they will humbly confess and ask the Lord to help them overcome this weakness. These are destiny moments in all of our lives.

Walk Like Christ

Every person who **says** they are a believer in Christ may not necessarily have been "born again." Some profess Christ who have never truly surrendered their lives to Him. They have only a head knowledge about Jesus, but they do not know Him. Their spirit has not been renewed by the Holy Spirit. Others may have experienced salvation with the Lord but remain under-developed in their spiritual faith walk. Their walk with the Lord has many inconsistences and compromises. I have personally witnessed people live fruitless lives, because they remain rooted in selfish attitudes.

Some couples attend church who are not married, living together and thinking nothing of it. Some will read their Bible and even have their favorite verses, but they live the same as the world even after they have said a "salvation prayer." Social drinking seems to be the norm among many professing Christians now days, and the progression of sin has become bolder within the established church. Homosexuality is welcomed with open arms in many congregations and denominations with the Bible being quoted to "prove" their point with scriptures such as "Do not judge" or "God is love."

Society today is busy creating a god in "their own image" instead of recognizing the God of the Bible. They want a god who overlooks sin and redefines the love of God to base passions without restraint thinking that as long as I am happy, God is happy.

We should always welcome people who are in bondage and reach out to them with the leading of the Holy Spirit. But never under any circumstance should we alter what the Word of God says. We should be about presenting the gospel that Jesus can set them free. How they respond to that message is not our responsibility but the Holy Spirit's. The attitude in which we do present the message is our responsibility. Remember, the Word of God is a sharp and powerful two-edged sword. It will do what it is sent to do.

The truth is people can remain in bondage thinking they are free and wondering why there is nothing but frustration in their lives. They are striving to create a utopian world where everything they desire is the focal point. Then, when their utopian world fails, they look for someone to blame. Those who are standing for uncompromising, biblical truth often become their target of choice.

All they are doing is watering the seeds of defeat in their own lives. Their very words and actions only produce more doubt, unbelief, anger, despair and bitterness in their hearts. These false imaginations are fruitless fig trees grown from the "destroying mountain" of the liar who is out to kill, steal and destroy everything good in their lives.

Offences will come

Another tactic used by our adversary is to have our biblical world view filtered through political correctness. I am not referring to legalism or the letter of the law but the pursuit of true biblical holiness that is produced by a hunger and desire to honor the Lord with our whole being.

Many people refuse to study and research what is being promoted through any given politician. I know we live in a fallen world, and there is no one in office who has it all right, and we are fortunate to have a voice in our political system. People say we should vote according to our own convictions. However, our convictions are nurtured by the kingdom from which we draw our life. Our voting decisions should be based on a biblical world view not on a personal world view. If the candidate we favor is a strong supporter of abortion and lifestyles that are clearly in opposition to scripture, and we vote them into office, then abortion and unbiblical lifestyles will be the order of the day. To claim to be a follower of Jesus and yet defend perversion and unholiness as acceptable, is not possible for a believer. God will never declare holy what He has already declared unholy. The deceiver will always plant a "false narrative" in your mind to believe a lie. That is a mountain that needs to come down.

God's word is very clear about the sanctity of life in the womb in Psalm 139, and children are a blessing from the Lord. God created male and female and ordained marriage as such. Because of an unbiblical view of scripture many have endorsed and aided the rise of ungodliness in the church, and they are not even aware of what the scripture says about their actions.

> *Romans 1:32*
> *"³² who, knowing the righteous judgment of God, that those who practice such things are deserving of death, not only do the same but **also approve of those who practice them.**"* (emphasis mine)

The sad truth is many have relegated the salvation experience to an insurance policy that gives them the assurance of Heaven after death. Our salvation experience should transform us into Christ's image. The Lord wants His light to shine forth through us to a dark world. Should He not receive the reward of His suffering? I am reminded of a quote by Lenard Ravenhill.

> *"You're saved? What are you saved from? Are you saved from lying, cheating, from being disobedient to your parents? Come on, tell me. What are you saved from?"*

This statement sums it all up. The salvation experience is a here and now work. Our ability to remove fruitless fig trees and mountains strongholds depends on which kingdom we are living in and manifesting daily. Realizing you were created for a divine purpose and good works should encourage you. The Lord has good works for you to do, and you are already prepared with all you need to do them. Let boldness and assurance be stirred up for the Lord has promised to never leave you nor forsake you.

Trusting

the

Plan

Chapter Ten

Our Family's Journey

The pathway to becoming "More than a Conqueror" will lead you through many diverse moments. It is part of the journey. The journey will have times of overwhelming joy. There will be days filled with boredom or filled with excitement. And there will be difficult times when your faith in God is tested beyond your limited endurance. In each of these moments you have a decision to make. Will you follow after the Lord or revert to a slave bondage mentality?

As a temple, a Holy Habitation of God, you have already been cleansed and brought to the waters of refreshing and set on the path of righteousness through salvation. Now comes the moment to choose what lives and what dies in your life. The journey you are on will involve death to everything that has controlled and robbed you of that for which God has created you. The Lord our Shepherd has prepared a table before you, and He pours the oil of healing into your life and fills your cup to overflowing. He surrounds you with strength and guidance from His Word (His staff) and His rod (sword of the Spirit for protection) as in Psalms 23. As you submit to the removal of each hindrance, our Father will expose your adversary and deliver your soul in the very presence of the one who has had you bound. You then become a living testimony declaring that Jesus defeated him and put him to an open shame.

Life's Journey to Inheritance

The following pages are mine and my family's journey through some of our destiny moments which saw the removal of fruitless fig trees and mountain strongholds in our own lives. Our Lord Jesus has brought us through many trials and joyous experiences. There have been times when great grief and fear gripped our hearts and times when the sweetness of His presence flooded our souls. Our victories and failures are submitted to show the amazing patience and grace of our Lord Jesus Christ as we run our race to the ever-present horizon before us. The encounters we have had with the Lord were of His choosing. How the Lord chooses to reveal Himself to you may be entirely different. The key is to seek and wait on Him. He will be found, and you will never forget the moment.

My wife and I and our children have nothing to boast about except in our Lord Jesus. We share these things as a testimony to the never-ending compassion and mercy of our Lord. Times of refreshing in God's presence have come, and His joy has always been our strength. We still face battles with our own personal, fruitless fig trees and mountain strongholds from time to time, and for each one of us it is a time of learning and growth. Some habits, strongholds and wrong ways of thinking have taken longer to remove than others. However, we can truthfully say we have seen a lot of fruitless trees destroyed and replaced with fruitful trees of blessings and strength for service. We have seen our Lord Jesus level the ground in many places in order to build us up into His Holy Habitation. Our only direction is forward to the Mountain of the Lord. My hope is that our life experiences will encourage you on your journey. There is light on your horizon and the fragrance of fresh fruit.

The Call

Let me begin with how the Lord set me on my path to becoming a holy habitation. I was raised in a Christian home, and I knew how to act around family and church people. But not really being born again, it was easy to be like my friends. I graduated from high school in June, 1970. My plans were to join the military, but the Lord had other plans.

The summer after graduation I went to a youth summer camp, and that is where everything changed. I was born again and baptized with the Holy Spirit on the first night of the week of church camp. I still had my plans to join the military, but I needed to get some personal things in order before enlisting. That was taking some time, but I was loving church. Being part of a strong, no-nonsense youth group was a tremendous help.

In the spring of 1971, I attended an early Sunday morning, men's prayer breakfast. As I was driving home, for the first time I heard the Lord speak to me. Yes, I heard His voice. Whether an audible voice coming through my physical ears or just in my heart, I do not know. His voice was clear and direct, and I knew it was the Lord as His Spirit always bears witness with our spirit. Even to this day I can remember every word, the exact location, and what the weather was like. He simply said, "I want you to go to L.I.F.E. Bible College and study the ministry for Me."

Some might ask, "How do you know it was God?" Simple. All my desire to join the military immediately vanished. When I arrived home, I told my parents God had called me into the ministry, and I was going to L.I.F.E. Bible College that fall. Believe me. They were in shock. Not because I was going to Bible college but because of the sudden change in my direction. They just knew it was right.

Here I want to be very clear. I had a lot of baggage, and God knew every piece in greater detail than I did. Yet, He still called me. I guess He likes a good project, and boy did He have one.

As I entered college with all of the excitement of being far away from home for the first time, it was a true adventure. I was from North Carolina going to a college in Los Angeles, California. It really was a culture shock for this country boy. I quickly found out that college is not like summer camp. You have classes with research and term papers, and with a part time job to boot, trying to balance a social life with new friends is not an easy task. This should be an indication that, even though called to the ministry, it really is a lot of hard work. However, the "vision" I had of ministry kept me going.

Planting Time and Missed Opportunities

God has ways of planting the seed of His purpose in us even when we do not realize what He is doing. In a chapel service of which I had a part, Pastor Bill Burnett Sr., the father of one of my classmates, stood and pointed to me and said, "The Lord is saying to you...

Isaiah 54:17
"17 No weapon formed against you shall prosper,
And every tongue which rises against you in judgment
you shall condemn. This is the heritage of the servants of
the LORD, and their righteousness is from Me, says
the LORD."

Being fairly new to the Pentecostal movement, I knew this was what happened occasionally, but I did not understand what it fully meant. Little did I know how the scripture seed planted in me on that day would carry a greater meaning. Fig trees and mountains are on the far horizon.

Also, being so new to most of this I did not know the names of many, well-known evangelists and powerful teachers of the word. One missed opportunity I had was to meet Kathryn Kuhlman. One weekend an announcement was made that a single lady needed help moving some large items, and about five of us volunteered. After we finished moving her, the lady informed us she was an assistant to Kathryn Kuhlman, and she invited us to attend the service where Kathryn was speaking. She said we would have front row seats and could meet Ms. Kuhlman afterwards. We all declined as we were too busy with other plans for the weekend. Lesson learned. Never be too busy.

Moving ahead to December, 1974 I married the most wonderful lady I had ever met, and at the time of this writing, 45 years later, I am more in love with Jan than ever. It was at our wedding rehearsal where I met a couple who sang and prophesied over us. John and Marcia Kendall would not only become wonderful friends over the years but would be instrumental in planting seeds of faith and encouragement. I still have a three-page letter they gave us in 1982 which I read often. Their words continue to encourage me to this day.

I cannot over emphasize the importance of strong, well-balanced friendships when you are on your journey. A timely phone call, a letter or invitation, and words from the Lord are invaluable and should not be taken lightly or ignored. But this too was a lesson I would have to learn.

Early Years of Ministry

Upon graduation in June of 1975 we embarked upon our life in ministry as youth pastors in Columbus, Georgia. We spent one year there then took our first pastorate in Longview, Texas. The church had been closed for a while, so there were not any people at first. It was there that God's provision and promise of Isaiah 54:17 would be a shield against the discouragements we would face. Over time we did gather a few people and began to do the best we knew how, and for the most part things went well.

Then one Monday morning as I was at work, Jan called me and said a couple was "just passing" through and needed some help financially, and what should she do? I knew we had received $89.00 in checks and cash the past Sunday. I told her to give them all the cash, and she responded, "All of it?" I said, "Yes." There was a little miscommunication here. She understood me to say ALL the money both the cash and the checks. So, in simple faith she did just that. When I got home, she informed me she had done as I had instructed by explaining her thoroughness in giving ALL the offering away. Needless to say, I did not handle it very well. Many times, we see ourselves as giants of faith, yet when the slightest dust storm arises it exposes our lack of fruit.

God is so good. The Lord knew this would happen and had already prepared a blessing for us. A Sunday School class over 900 miles away on the very same Sunday of that week, had been led to receive an offering for our tiny church. The offering came to $389.00. The Lord was exposing the fig trees of self-reliance, doubt and fear. I was on a journey of learning, and He would expose just how deep those roots were.

With the birth of our daughter, Hannah Marie, in November of 1976, we took a position as youth pastors in Brownfield, Texas. We remained there until the spring of 1980 after the birth of our oldest son, Travis Duane, the previous September, 1979. From there we left full time ministry for a season and moved to Rockwall, Texas.

While living in Rockwall, we spoke at area churches upon request and filled in for pastors on vacation. We were also able to have more fellowship with John and Marcia while living in the Dallas area. Here would come another missed opportunity that I felt too busy to attend, or should I say, was afraid to attend.

Marcia, who is the founder of Flame Fellowship International, was having their annual banquet in Dallas. The guest speaker was Evangelist and Prophet Lester Sumrall, and she wanted Jan and I to sit next to him during the meal before he spoke. He had spent time in England when he was a young man and had become a close, personal friend of Smith Wigglesworth. Needless to say, this was a tremendous honor. But I was also aware of some fruitless fig trees the Lord had pointed out, and I was not so sure about meeting the man of God at that moment. By allowing my own thoughts and voices of fear from the past to control my decision, the adversary was successful in keeping me away. This robbed both Jan and me of possible enrichments in our lives. Our choices do affect others.

While in Rockwall Jan gave birth to our third child, Talmadge Paul, in February of 1982. Three years later we would move to Lubbock, Texas to pastor a small congregation of believers and assist them in relocating to a new facility.

School Is Now in Session

With the move coming up, we put our house on the market and took a trip to Lubbock to see about purchasing a house since the church did not own a parsonage. We felt rushed but needed a place. We looked all of one day and put five hundred dollars down on a house with the understanding that our house would have to sell by a certain date. Neither of us felt good about what we had done, but what else could we do? We each had an uneasy feeling about it but had not shared it with the other. God had a plan, and at two o'clock in the morning the Lord woke us both up. We knew we had acted in haste and fear. We knew we needed to repent, and as we prayed and asked for forgiveness, we both heard in our spirit these words, "You have seen what you can do. Now, let Me show you what I can do." In less than a month we were provided with a brand-new, brick home just three blocks from the place the new church would be built. The most exciting part of all was this brand-new home was completely paid for and ours to use for the church. This meant we did not have to pay rent. God is so good, and His plan is so much better than ours. With all of that behind us, being a pastor was the order of the day. We only had a few people at first, but they were faithful and were always supportive.

Not long after we entered the new building, I went on a seven day fast. On the third day as I was rushing into the sanctuary for my time of prayer, an angel (unseen) reached out his hand and forcefully pressed it against my chest and said, "Slow down. He is here." This was a defining and an awakening moment. Nothing like this had ever happened to me before, and after that encounter, the realm of the spirit became more real than I had ever known. I believe we can pray anywhere and at any time during any activity. But there is no prayer time as powerful and engaging as having a designated time in a quiet place with the door shut. In these moments the Lord can speak to your heart as you receive hearing ears and seeing eyes. These can only be imparted when there are no other distractions. He sees your overall journey and the destiny moments you will face. The quiet place is designed to impower you for the days ahead.

It was during this time that I had my first face to face encounter with demonic spirits. The Lord had me in school, and this was the real deal. The only thing that can prepare you for this is the Holy Spirit. I will relate only one, but there were others. The last day of the fast was a Sunday. We had finished the service and gone home. Jan was preparing lunch for her and the children. I went to the bedroom and closed the door and was thinking of all the spiritual encounters of the week. I was very much awake when a blackness engulfed me. There appeared before me the face of a creature gangrene in color and whose face was distorted. It was laughing and mocking me for the fast and prayer time of that week. He spoke and said, "Who do you think you are?" Then the Lord brought to my mind Micah 7:8, *"Laugh not at me, my enemy. When I fall, I will arise. When I sit in darkness, the Lord will be my Light."* With that I spoke back. "Be gone in the name of Jesus," and immediately it vanished.

Before I move on, I want to mention. Your encounters in prayer may be much different. The Lord chooses how and when He will engage us. Our responsibility is to seek Him. These types of experiences do not happen every time, but when they do, there is a specific reason. Learn from that moment but do not put down roots and stay in that place. In those times He is planting something deep within your spirit to prepare you for your destination and inheritance.

God is interested in you, your trees and your mountains. We all have them, and we each face them one at a time. He is in charge of the school and reveals what is necessary and when. So be ready. He has a way of doing the unexpected.

During our four-year period in Lubbock, we had some interesting, learning experiences. Each one had its own lesson to teach us and revealed a weakness or fear that needed to be confronted. Understand that the journey is not all work. We had unexpected blessings, victories, spiritual growth and rest along the way. We have very fond memories of our time in Lubbock. The Lord knows how to lead you and heal you when you are not even aware.

One Sunday morning a couple walked into the church that I had never seen. After the service the man confessed to me that he was gripped with an alcoholic spirit. He and his wife both said he could stay drunk for a full six months at a time. And to get sober, it could take as long as a month after he stopped the drinking. What he and his wife told me next was quite an eye-opener. He said that God spoke to him while he was still drunk and said, "If you will go to that little church down the street, I will deliver you from alcohol." God was true to His word, and in a few months' time he was totally delivered. This opened a door of ministry to their entire family which then led to a home group meeting with her invalid mother.

Another event that happened during our time in Lubbock was when our youngest son had a major ear infection, but he still wanted to go to his kindergarten class. We did not have the income at the time to afford a doctor, so prayer was our resource. When I picked him up at noon, he was full of energy as if nothing was wrong. Indeed, nothing was wrong. His teacher told me that at around 9:30 all this fluid started draining from his ear. It was at that exact time I had been praying and asking the Lord to heal my son.

During our time in Lubbock, Jan was working at a small, Christian school as a teacher. We received free tuition and a small salary for her work. In fact, the salary had gotten so small that for some time the money was not there to be paid. At least the free tuition was a blessing. Christmas was just a few weeks away, and the school was doing a food drive for nonperishable food. Our three children wanted to take something, but the only thing we had was a few boxes of Mac and Cheese and canned beans. When I say that was all, I mean that was all we had left, but the children were happy to help out. You may be tempted to say, "Well, what was your problem that you could not do better?" My answer is this. God has a plan. We stepped out to follow His plan even when things did not make sense to our natural understanding.

That morning as the children left for school with their gift for a needy family, a vanload of young people from Brownfield, Texas was on their way to Lubbock on a mission. It was an early release day from school, and when Jan and the children returned home, there was a church van parked in our driveway unloading several hundred pounds of groceries. I do not mean dented cans or leftovers of almost expired food but fresh beef, chicken, turkey, and everything in-between. God has a plan.

Something Special

As you might have already surmised, our time in Lubbock was without any regular income. It was tough at times especially around Christmas with three small children. We just assured them they would all receive something for Christmas, so let us be thankful for all the food and nice warm house that had been provided. Really, we knew it would not be too bad for them, as we knew they would receive gifts from both sets of grandparents. But as their parents we were a bit sorrowful, because we wanted to get them something as well.

We really did have fun during those lean months. We would take all the mattresses off the bed and put them on the floor in front of the fireplace. We ate popcorn and listened to missionary stories from Moody Bible Radio Church on the house intercom system. We were high tech! Even with that encouragement you could see the disappointment in our children's eyes. We were following the Lord as best we knew how, and things were a little hard at times. Have you ever been in that place where you just wonder if the Lord is really there? We need to remember. God has a plan.

About five days before Christmas we were able to show our children God's faithfulness in a very tangible way. As I checked the mail, there were a few Christmas cards from friends and one from our sister church across town. In this card was a check for $350.00. That puts a spring in your step. The next day seemed brighter and Christmas more real than we had remembered. Sometimes when you have an overabundance, it is easy to become complacent. Waiting and trusting is part of the School of the Spirit for it reveals fig trees and mountains, and it is also training for bigger mountains. God chooses how and when He will move and for what purpose.

The very next day another Christmas card came from some friends we had not heard from in some time. In the card was a check for $2400.00. Wow, that was a total of $2750.00 in two days! No one knew anything about our income, but God did, and He had a plan. We tithed to our own church on those funds which helped pay the utility bills, but we wanted to help someone else. Jan knew of a young pastor and his family who had left the ministry because of discouragement. They were in a dire situation and basically had nothing. We took the opportunity God had given to teach our children to reach out to others. We were able to go to the local meat market and purchase a 40-pound box of meat to give them along with a check of $250.00 from our blessings. These things are not being said to boast but to show God how works through people. His plan is for everyone to be His hand extended. Little did we know how these acts of kindness would also be seeds planted in our children's lives for later years, when they would face their own fig trees and mountains.

When our youngest son was five, a friend of mine from Dallas called and asked if I could come and work for a month. I accepted the job, and Talmadge went with me. Jan's parents lived in Garland so we stayed there. I was working some long hours and only saw Talmadge twice during the whole month as he would be in bed when I got in. One day his grandmother asked him if he had seen his dad. Talmadge said, "No, but I felt him once." God is always there even if we do not see him. If we are quiet, we will feel him too.

Our time in Lubbock would eventually end, and we would move on. The memories of our time there are very precious, but God was not through. A large fig tree and mountain of pride was about to be exposed.

Who Owns This?

With my background in construction, coming to Lubbock was a good fit. It was my total responsibility to find land and oversee the construction of a new facility. The biggest problem I had was gradually taking ownership of the whole project and seeing it as "my" church and wanting it to be done my way.

About a year after the completion of the new facility, I felt it was time to leave Lubbock. Upon learning we were leaving, our sister church wanted to merge the two congregations and take possession of the property, so they could relocate into the newer facility. Permission was granted, and upon our leaving they were able move forward with merging the two congregations. To put it mildly, I was not at all pleased with this arrangement. Other than a Christmas card with some money what had they contributed to this project? The Lord brought to my attention this attitude of mine, yet was very gracious in His approach. He asked me this simple question, "Do you know what a steward is?" I said, "Yes, a steward is basically one who handles the affairs of the rightful owner and does as the rightful owner desires." The Lord responded, "That is correct, and who owns this property and all that is on it?" I said, "You do, Lord." That was the end of the matter, and through that simple conversation and repentance a fig tree and mountain were removed.

I can truthfully say God can do anything He wants with what is His. That includes all those He has bought with His blood. We are His rightful possession, and where He places us will always be right.

Crash Course

Our next move was short lived. We were only there for six months. During that time our son, Travis, who was ten, had a fall from a horse and broke his femur. This left him in the hospital in traction for six weeks and then in a body cast for another six weeks. All total Travis was homebound for 6 months before he was allowed to attend school. Talmadge also broke two fingers at school the same year. It was a rough six months.

Then, I received a call from my supervisor, Dr. Sydney Westbrook, informing us that he wanted us to move to Abilene, Texas. Later, after the move, he told us we had learned more in six months than many pastors learn in a lifetime. It was like a crash course. Whew! Glad it didn't last any longer than six months. There were other factors involved, but he felt Abilene would be a good place to be. Indeed, Abilene was a good place for us. Being next to our church, camp-ground facilities afforded many summer job opportunities for our boys. The church had a K-12 Christian school which was a lot of hard work, but it was also very rewarding. However, God knew more pruning was needed.

The fig trees and mountains we were going to encounter in our fast-approaching horizon would be faced with a loving group of people, and that was God's gift to us. Isaiah 54:17 would become a main stay in the coming years, yet its full potential was still to be revealed. It was in Abilene where God had chosen to do major tree removal and mountain levelling.

Old Growth

Our lives and emotions are strongly influenced by outside forces. Words, attitudes, or how others look at us with approval or disapproval can become a snare. Being raised in a Christian home does not mean every word or response will be edifying. My parents were very loving, and my sister, Teresa, and I lacked for nothing. Our parents were not perfect parents nor were Jan and I perfect parents. Our parents passed on methods of motivation that were passed on to them, and we in many ways did the same. There was no physical abuse, but I was many times "shamed" for failure. Please do not read into this any animosity towards my parents. There is none. Even knowing how much love they had for me, the words that were spoken were shaping me. My personality was being developed to respond to the tone of voice or "the look," and I was learning to retreat from strong personalities. These traits many times become generational and can become mountains that manifest in many ways. Even when I felt I had something to contribute, I often refrained from doing so for fear of rejection. Having a quiet personality and using "my quietness" as an excuse was, in truth, a fig tree grown from the mountain of failure. And living in perceived failure will never produce life.

Looking back on this I remembered a moment in the eighth grade. My sister, who is five years older and extremely smart, has achieved much in nursing as an adult. During our school years, we had the same science teacher. I was not as studious as my sister as I always desired more hands-on activities and struggled more with formulas and so forth than she did. One morning in class I had not grasped a concept as quickly as the teacher required, and in front of the class she asked, "J.D., why are you not as smart as Teresa?" I can still remember the sting of those words and in response to them being spoken, I just stared and said nothing. Most in the class thought it was funny, and that just solidified those comments. My only response was to close my book and refuse to open it again. Rebellion or deep hurt? Both probably. Because of my refusal to open my book again, I even refused to take any tests. Why should I? I would just fail, so why even try? She called in my parents, but even that did not motivate me to try.

The words were already taking root, and the adversary moved quickly to reinforce those words with line upon line of failure. I was labeled "not smart enough" and would always be compared to the great achievers in the family, who have gone on to tremendous productive lives. To this day I think very highly of my sister and her achievements. She is an inspiration to me and has always been supportive of her younger brother.

It has taken years to be rid of this tree and mountain. Even graduating from college with a Bachelor of Arts Degree did not help to remove the root of those words. After all these years of public speaking, the adversary still shoots that fiery dart and at times stirs up those old emotions. This should confirm God's word as true. We are in a spiritual war, and only the weapons of the Holy Spirit are sufficient to defeat this destroying mountain. The scripture is clear. *"Death and Life are in the power of the tongue, and you will eat of its fruit."* Proverbs 18:21

Voices from the Past

We found in Abilene a wonderful group of people, not perfect, but a well-balanced congregation and faithful. The biggest issue we faced was a debt of $160,000.00 with an average attendance of 30-35 when we arrived. Along with that the church had a K-12 private school. Throw parents into the mix, and things could become interesting in many ways. Our small salary of $125.00 a week with a family of five made it necessary to have outside employment. I had a background in construction, so I would do odd jobs always making sure I was free for the church.

Because of the tightness of the budget our monthly council meetings could be very stressful. Though none of it was personal, I often stepped back into the "safety" of the shadows and would not take the lead. I was the pastor and should have done so, but with the huge task being faced and stronger voices prevailing, in my eyes, I failed. Then came the attack of the adversary saying, "God called YOU? I don't think so. You have failed at everything. Why should you think it will be different here?" The old voices from the past and of false humility, which is a disguise for weakness and pain, were a constant companion. Yet on Sunday mornings, I put on the "pastor" face and did what pastors do. I would be "strong" while all along dying on the inside. Fig leaves are extremely heavy, and they can crush the life out of you, and the mountain they grow from is more than eager to add to the load.

> NOTE: This part is my wife's words. *"It is amazing how we can believe the lie of our adversary during weak or stressful moments. I think we can all relate. JD was*

such an amazing pastor. Ask anyone. His preaching was passionate and deep, and everyone to this day recalls his pastor's heart. He was always there for us, and we learned so much under his preaching. Even many in my extended family have said they have not heard any preacher as good as their Uncle JD. He is a very godly man and full of wisdom. He is my love and my life."

We may deal with little sprouts along the way, but eventually the root has to come out and the mountain be removed. Over the years the Lord had manifested much grace and mercy to my family as we moved from town to town. But we came to Abilene to stay and in doing so, the fig trees and mountains would have to be faced.

The journey and destiny moments we face in the removal of strongholds are for the birthing of deep spiritual works of the Spirit. They do not make sense to the natural man and many times are quite painful. We live in a fallen and broken world, and being a child of God does not exempt you from difficult times. But in these times, He gives a very special grace that words cannot describe. On this journey we call life we will face moments of deep darkness where we have to choose between "life" or "death." Do I keep my eyes on Jesus and let Him comfort and strengthen, or do I become an accuser and live in bitterness? There can be sudden events that happen in life which will continue to define who you are for years after they occur. How they define you depends on how you respond to them. The things that our family faced are still defining who we are.

Deepest Heartache

Our fellowship was small in Abilene when we arrived but had grown to around 75 people by our eighth year and ranged from toddlers to 70 and 80-year old's. There had not been one death in our aging congregation up to this point. At times I wondered who would be my first funeral here. Not that I wanted it to happen, but it just came with being observant of the fellowship. Little did I know who it would be.

On November 12, 1998 at 1:30 pm our youngest son, Talmadge Paul, was in a single car accident and went to be with Jesus at age 16. He was a student at our Christian school, and his mother was the school administrator. Talmadge had forgotten his lunch and wanted to go back home to get it. We lived twelve miles from the school at the time, but mom allowed him to go. On his way back it began to rain. As he approached a slight curve, his car went into a skid. He over corrected and slid into the guard rail and flipped his car. At the school the students were outside on lunch break. Our eldest son, Travis, was shooting basketballs when the Care Flight Helicopter flew over the school. As Travis looked up a voice told him, "It is going to get Talmadge." Travis thought it was just a crazy thought and blew it off. By the time the hospital called the school, Talmadge was already in the presence of the Lord.

Everything comes to a sudden stop. No warning. All of the plans, whether family or church, suddenly changes direction, and nothing and I mean nothing will ever be the same.

Talmadge was a typical teenage boy in many ways. He was goofy at times making everyone laugh at his antics. He was learning to play the guitar and was part of the worship team at church, and he played the trumpet in the school band. This was going to impact a lot of lives. As someone later put it, "If you had a down day, Talmadge could always make you feel better, because he could always make you laugh." The devastation of this event affected so many of his friends. Notes and letters started pouring in from all over the state from pastors and youth groups who knew Talmadge from church camp. Youth pastors took the opportunity to speak about eternity to their youth groups, and many lives were changed. But time somehow moves forward, and we began trying to put our lives back together.

Being Carried

Then the mountain starts talking to you, and the accusations start coming like a massive flash flood, and you find all your strength gone. Also, out of this tragedy the seeds of added discontentment were being planted in our oldest son, Travis. More lay ahead, and it did not take long.

I was in Dallas at the time working on a project with my friend, Pastor Robbie Moore, when Jan called and told me what had happened. When I got off of the phone, I told Robbie and immediately I said, "I must have done something wrong. That is why this happened." Suddenness can cause you to fall back on your own strength, but Pastor Robbie stepped in and hugged me and said, "NO!" and began to pray and bind that attitude.

This could not be happening. Talmadge is just 16. This is not right. This is the moment, in physical death, that the life and strength of Jesus is found in other believers, and they carry you. When the Lord steps in with His comfort, the taunts from the mountain have to be silent. Strength was coming from many sources, not only from our church family but from pastors and churches all over the country. The Lord had prepared so much help and covering for us, and He had them ready to step in at the right time.

Do Not Doubt God's Care

Some might ask, "If God is so prepared, why did Talmadge die? Doesn't Isaiah 54:17 say that no weapon formed against you shall prosper? To ask this question is the same as in the garden when Satan asked Eve, *"Has God indeed said?"* Genesis 3:1. Because of the quick response of praying people, we could stand against the adversary's accusations and would not allow the darkness to define God's eternal Word. This is not an easy task. All of our physical beings were under siege. It is a daily struggle more often than not. During times of discouragement it can be a challenge to keep our minds focused on the eternal perspective. As God's people we are not exempt from hardships in this life. But in these times, we have a choice to walk by faith and trust or to become an accuser. Even now, over 20 years later, the sorrow of loss can grip our hearts, and we again must choose to trust. We must not ever allow the darkness to define God or His eternal Word. The choices we make will have eternal consequences. Choosing to lean on the Lord even in darkness is light to the soul.

There are things that happen that I do not understand, but to doubt God's care and compassion is not part of it. I want to mention here that even on our best day we fall short and must depend on God's grace. This tragedy was **not** ordained by God for punishment. Being born of His Spirit does not give us a "get out of tragedy" free card. We live in a very broken world, and when the suddenness of life hits, we have someone bigger to lean on. When this happened, the Lord was not removing anything spiritually from us. We may not have seen it at the time, and we did not know it, but a deeper, inner strength was being birthed. It does not lessen the emotional pain and sense of loss, but our Lord Jesus has ways of bringing comfort, and He chooses how to minister it. We were created for good works and to be His hand extended here on Earth.

Gifts of Comfort

I will now recount what happened to our daughter when she received word of Talmadge. She and her husband were living at Fort Jackson Army Post in Columbia, South Carolina. The sudden shock took her breath, and she went to the bathroom to wash her face with cold water. As she looked into the mirror, it vanished away, and she was looking through a mist. As it cleared Talmadge was sitting on green grass with someone standing next to him in a long white robe. Talmadge looked at her with a smile and said, "Hannah, I'm alright. It didn't hurt. Tell mom and dad I love them and in about (?) years you will all be with me." Some might say this was just her grief, except for the next thing she saw. Hannah said, "Dad, Talmadge had a neckless made from a white stone, and something was written on the stone, but I couldn't read it." I knew immediately what she saw was true. I ask her, "Do you know what Revelation 2:17 says?" She replied, "No."

> *Revelation 2:17* (emphasis mine)
> *"He who has an ear, let him hear what the Spirit says to the churches. To him who overcomes I will give some of the hidden manna to eat.* ***And I will give him a white***

stone, and on the stone a new name written which no one knows except him who receives it."

On the night of the accident we cried out in prayer, not asking why but for strength, and we asked the Lord to do something for us. I said, "Lord, I don't know if you do this or not, but if you would, tell Talmadge we love him and miss him." About six weeks later while I was studying for my Sunday morning message the presence of the Lord came into the room. When I say He came, I mean He Came! The air was thick but not burdensome, and I got very still, and the Lord whispered in my ear, "Talmadge said to tell you he loves you too."

The Lord has confirmed through signs and wonders with the gentleness of His presence that He cares. He touched me in the darkness. Talmadge is not in our past. He is in our future. God has a plan.

The Good Shepherd

It may be hard to understand, but through all of this God was strengthening us for other mountains we would face. I have learned that many times fruitless fig trees and mountain strongholds will be removed by walking and speaking in obedience to the living Word of God. In fact, you may not realize they are gone until you move on. This is the expressed grace and mercy of God. We are to confront our fruitless trees and mountain strongholds. That is the purpose of the journey. When the wounds are fresh and the bruises deep, the Good Shepherd anoints our wounds, and while we rest, a fig tree and mountain is removed. He not only ministers His peace and healing for the moment. He sees much, much deeper, and He is going to reach to the depths of our lives and break every chain.

That is really what God asked Israel to do when they left Egypt. He says, "I will be your Shepherd. Walk and speak in obedience to my Word, and I will bring you to completeness. You will bring down giants and inherit the promise."

The Encounter

In January 1999, two months after the Talmadge's accident, our church was involved in a joint church service in Wichita Falls, Texas. I was physically there but not mentally. During the praise and worship, as everyone was standing except me, the Lord asked me very gently, "Will you trust Me?" I did not know what to say. I thought I was trusting. I was believing and had faith. Are they not the same thing? Little did I realize the significance of His question. The Father was watering His Word (seed) which had been planted in my spirit many years earlier and was leading me to a deeper understanding of trust. He knew many other days ahead would be stormy. Yet, other days would hold much sunshine. He is true to His word, *"I'll never leave you, nor forsake you."* He sees the deep hidden areas of our heart, and what He saw in me was a little boy trembling with fear and uncertainty under the crushing weight of sorrow. My faith was under assault. Even with all of the assurances He had already given questions still remained. What happens now? How do we live? Psalm 56:3 *"When I am afraid, I will trust in You."* But HOW do you do that? As I sat there silently on the pew while everyone else around me in the service was singing, I felt His presence. He said nothing else beyond, "Will you trust Me?" He was silent waiting for my response. In my mind it seemed He started walking, then stopped, turned and looked at me as if to say, "Well, what are you going to do?" What could I do? My emotions were raw. I chose to walk after Him. Where was He going? I did not know, but it had to be better than the place I was in. His healing presence did not stop at that moment. It is a river, a continuous flowing river, and He invites you and me to enter the deep waters of His Spirit.

During this time, it was the faith and prayers of God's people that gave us the comfort everything would be alright. But we had just started this part of our journey, and all of our emotions and beliefs were under attack. Fiery darts were being shot at us daily, and the adversary never takes a day off. He loves to attack when we are at our weakest, but it is in our weakness that the Lord's strength is made perfect. I had been placed into a teaching and training period that would last twenty years. Learning to trust was to be the catalyst for my coming destination and living in my inheritance.

Everyday Trust

We live in a world where perception is everything. Being a pastor makes it possible for the adversary to really pile it on. I wanted to be strong but for all the wrong reasons. I was the pastor called by God. I may be wounded, but I will be what pastors are supposed to be - STRONG.

The Lord sees it all, and He is not angry, just purposeful in His leading. What I say now was lived out, little by little, over the next twenty years in many ways that has brought Jan and I freedom, and it is ever expanding.

The Sunday before Talmadge went to be with Jesus, I spoke from the text in John 6 of the feeding of the 5,000, where the little boy gave his five barley loaves and two fish to

Jesus. Verse 6 says, *"There is a lad who has five barley loaves and two small fish, but what are they among so many?"* For some reason Talmadge wrote this verse on a scrap piece of paper and put it into his wallet. We found it as we went through his personal items. Not long afterwards we were given a quote by Elizabeth Elliot that says, *"If my life is broken when given to Jesus, it is because pieces will feed a multitude, while a loaf will satisfy only a little lad."*

We all come face to face with our inadequacies and face the choice of living a pretentious life or lifting all our brokenness and lack to the Father and being thankful. At these times we are not being asked about our faith. We are being asked about our trust. As we give it all to Him, we will receive back - abundance for lack, healing for pain, and strength for weakness. The Father's response will encompass every area of our lives - body, soul, and spirit.

At times it may seem more difficult to live in a place of surrender to His will, but the rewards are far greater. With that being said, I still face choices every day. My goal is to always make the righteous choice. Only His ways can produce life and abundance.

Fiery Darts

Travis and Talmadge were typical brothers, fighting, running around together, arguing about many things, but they did love each other. Their personalities were very different. I could see in Travis much of myself at that age. I had used many of the parenting skills used on me. Some were good and others not so good, and I had passed them on to my own children. This would eventually come to a head in Travis as he walked away from God, and the death of his brother only accelerated the process. The next ten years were in some ways more difficult to walk through than the death of Talmadge. Many may find that a strange statement, but in death when a person is with Jesus, we have the future and all of eternity to enjoy. But when your child walks away from all that is right and lives in open rebellion, the anxiety and emotional battle is a living nightmare. There is no amount of talking or reasoning that will work.

We prayed, cried, rebuked and did everything we knew to do, and it all seemed to fall short. Then in the middle of all of this our daughter and her husband divorced. Her life went into a tailspin while living in South Carolina, and it was made more difficult with us living in Texas.

All the while the voice of the adversary was saying, "I thought you were victorious; a pastor and you could not even manage your own family. What gives you the right to preach when your own family is in such a mess?"

The adversary has destroyed many good pastors with these same words, and much of it comes from unrealistic ideas about pastors. Often the church sees them as being perfect and not having parenting issues or "real" problems at all. When something like this happens, he is soundly criticized and not held up in prayer, and much too often it breeds death to his calling. However, Jan and I were very blessed to be the pastors of a loving group of people who were very supportive and held us up in prayer. We could not have made it through without them.

When You Least Expect It

The Lord knew everything that was happening, and He visited me in a way I never expected. His timing is always perfect even when it does not make sense to our way of thinking. Jesus was well aware of the taunting and accusing words of the adversary, and in the early hours of Resurrection Sunday, 2004 God showed up. I was coming out of a deep sleep but not quite awake. During these times I am more sensitive to the spirit realm for the busyness of the day has not cluttered my thoughts. There was singing off in the distance, and it was slowly coming closer. I awoke with Jesus singing over me the words to the song, "Draw Me Close to You."

> *Zephaniah 3:17*
> *"17 The LORD your God in your midst,*
> *The Mighty One, will save;*
> *He will rejoice over you with gladness,*
> *He will quiet you with His love,*
> *He will rejoice over you with singing."*

I was taken back and began to tell Him He should not be singing that song to me. I should sing it to Him. Then He began to explain the words to me. If you are familiar with the song, you will understand. The words are, "Draw me close to you; Never let me go; I'd lay it all down again; to hear you say that I'm your friend; You are My desire; No one else will do." I had always taken the words to be about me laying down all I have to follow Jesus. But He explained that no matter how much I laid down; it would never be enough to be His friend. His friendship cannot be bought with anything or any amount of work. He simply asks us to receive what He has freely given by His sacrifice.

What Jesus was saying is our friendship is precious to Him, so precious that He would go through every pain again just to hear His people say we are His friends. When He speaks to you, His full attention is on you and the things that concern you. You mean that much to Him. What spoke to me the most was that He knew I was still facing many issues in my life, and He was there to see me through. He was fully committed to fulfilling the divine purpose for which I was created. This is His heart for all those He has redeemed.

Unexpected Blessings

In 2006 the Lord blessed the church with three sizable, monetary gifts to pay off our debt. Sixteen years after moving to Abilene the load was finally gone. As I was thanking the Lord for this blessing, I asked what was next? He said, "You are not going to be here. You have done what I sent you here to do." The word steward became more real that day. What was I to do?

Over the next year I began preparing the church for our departure. They did not realize the sermons were directed to slowly prepare them. We were blessed to have a fellowship in unity with an average attendance of 100-125, and they were finally completely out of debt. On the first Sunday of July, 2007 after seventeen years I announced our leaving. It was a shock to all, but it was time.

I'm Just Being Responsible

One great biblical truth and principle instilled in me while growing up was to pay your bills and never be late under any circumstance. A good name is better to be had than riches, and a good credit score is a must. Now this may be true. However, it was so true in my life that it became an idol of pride, of which I was humbly proud. I did not see it at the time, because the Bible says we should have a good name, so I was just obeying God as I saw it.

You can dress an idol up in all kinds of scripture, but it is still an idol. And the Lord will not have it in your life, nor will He allow you to twist His word to justify it being in your life. The first time the Word of God was twisted was back in the garden and look what happened to humanity.

This idol I had cherished all of my adult life was about to be brought down. I am so thankful for the spiritual insight of a godly wife. One day she flat out told me that I had an idol in my life. I thought she was just finding fault when she said, "You have made your credit score an idol!" I argued that having a credit score of 830 was a good name, and it was biblical. I was to learn that you can justify anything, even an idol, with scripture.

After resigning from the church, we still needed to make a living. So, I bought a big truck and trailer and began hauling oilfield pipe and building material as an owner operator. When the oilfield went bust, I kept things going with credit cards. That got out of hand very fast. Loads dropped off, pay rates fell, and the credit score god was about to come crashing down. When the lower half of my truck engine went bad and it was going to cost $10,000 to repair, I was done. Add to this, we were $120,000.00 in debt with two house loans and a car loan, not to mention the credit cards. This all took place from 2007 until the summer of 2010. We were paying tithes and doing what we could. But we had ignored other biblical principles concerning finances. We had allowed ourselves to get way too much in debt and had not changed our spending habits, so it just got worse. We prayed and were faithful to tithe, but we did not do all that the lesson required. We needed to face the problem we had created and repent.

After we began walking in obedience, God spoke. He told us to write down everything we owed and to whom. That is painful in and of itself, but obedience is the key to breakthrough. He also reminded us of the power of our speech and instructed us to speak and prophecy over every offering we gave and over every bill. Change did not happen instantly. This is all seed sowing in the physical and the spiritual. Remember, salvation is instant, but sanctification takes time, and the process will be different for each person. Once that was done, a peace slowly began to settle. I can truthfully say that when you reach the place of God's peace, storms are not as menacing.

Breakthroughs Came Through Harder Circumstances

In 2008 Jesus moved in with His almighty power to pull Travis out of the pit, and He changed him in such a profound way that words are not adequate to describe the transformation. Our Lord will use any means necessary to reach a lost soul. In Travis' case, it was in the deep love for his daughter that the Lord revealed Himself. Travis realized the vileness of his life and recognized he needed to return to the Lord. The only way to redemption was brokenness and repentance, and things have never been the same since that night.

Travis had fathered a daughter in October of 2007 by his girlfriend, but their relationship did not last very long. The legal battles he was involved in were extremely stressful. Praying through the issues was very difficult, but that was part of the removal of fruitless fig trees and mountain strongholds. When all of this began, Travis took his responsibility as a father very serious. He stopped all social activity and went back to school. He moved back home and literally sold everything he owned to cover legal fees. He sold all his household goods, his movies and guitars, his motorcycle and even an old motorhome he worked out of. While it took many more prayers through even more stressful circumstances, we began to see the Lord rebuild our son's life and heal his personality.

Never give up on the Lord. Even prayers prayed in desperation and deep sorrow with many tears, do not go unnoticed. Travis was living with us, working part time, and going to school full time to get his FAA A&P license to work on airplanes. His child support payments were not large, but he paid each one faithfully, because he wanted to show he could take care of his daughter no matter what. He had another court date, and as he prepared for it the Lord told me, "Travis will never pay child support again." I told Travis this, but when he went to the hearing, the judge **raised** his child support. Needless to say, my son was very upset with me. But God does not lie and had a plan. Within six weeks Travis was summoned back to court. Not only did his child support payments stop, but he was granted primary custody. This meant his daughter now lived with him, and he received child support. His daughter was almost three at the time and has been in his primary care ever since.

During this time period, the Lord spoke to Travis' heart about going to South Africa for a men's conference. He was still in college, and the conference was in the middle of the semester. It did not look like there would be any way for him to miss without losing credit for those classes. For six months Travis said over and over again, "I am going to this Mighty Men's Conference in South Africa." He did not look at the seemingly, impossible obstacles. In January he was feeling a little down, because he did not have the money to purchase the airfare, nor did it look like he could miss a week's worth of A&P classes without losing credit for them. The Lord spoke, "Well, you have money for your passport, don't you?" So, in faith and in obedience Travis got his passport. With the conference in March he still needed money for airfare and provisions, but most of all he needed time off from his college classes. A few weeks prior to the conference, the professors decided to allow the students an extra week off so they could attend staff training. It just so happened it was the same week as the Mighty Men's Conference in South Africa. Praise the Lord!

The Robbery

We planned a garage sale to raise money for Travis' trip. We had sold a few items before the weekend of the sale, and Travis had $200 in a jar in his bedroom. On Thursday, the day before the sale, we had a break-in at our house. It had been raining that morning so the dogs were left in the utility room. Jan went home from work during her lunch hour to let them out and have a bit of lunch. When she opened the door to let them out, our dog, Sonny, ran to the back bathroom and started barking at the door. Jan thought he was just looking for me, and she insisted he go outside. He obeyed, and she went about her lunch. About 30 minutes after she left to go back to work, I came home and found the front door partly open. My first thought was that she had not closed front door tightly, and the wind blew it open. Then I saw a leg opening the door wider and thought, what is Travis doing home at this time of day not even thinking that his car was not there. You just do not think you are being robbed. Then I heard a crash as the burglar dropped our computer and rush toward the back door. Then it dawned on me what was happening. I chased him, but he had already bolted out the back door and over the fence. The house was ransacked. He had done a quick job. I also found dirty footprints in the bathroom tub. The burglar had been hiding in the tub at the time Jan was home for lunch which is why Sonny ran to the bathroom door. When I came home, I caught him in the act but didn't see his face so the police were not able to apprehend him. Praise the Lord for His protection. The only thing the burglar took was the $200.00, but this was not the only miracle that weekend.

Now, we have had garage sales in the past, and we usually made around $200-300. However, by the end of this weekend Travis had $2700.00. I am still amazed at how that happened. Obviously, it was a God thing. Travis purchased his plane ticket, went on his trip to South Africa, and had an amazing time with other men from all over the world. He shared his testimony with many and made lifetime friends. God is so good. Some of those good seeds that were planted when he was young were coming to fruition.

Remember, our words are seed, and they are powerful. The tender mercies of the Lord were carrying us through. The spiritual climate was tense at times, but words prayed and watered with tears put down deep roots. And when they break through, get ready, get ready, get ready, a harvest is coming!

It must be pointed out the Lord did not do this without us walking in obedience. He has requirements, and they must be followed no matter how difficult. Ours was continued prayer throughout difficult situations, and it took deep soul searching on our part. This was not an easy task. There were days of great bitterness, but this was and is part of the process of removing barren trees and mountain strongholds.

The Sun is Shining

By this time my credit god had been toppled, and I could no longer pay the credit cards. It was a huge amount, and I began to get the dreaded phone calls. At first, I was angry but quickly realized they had not done this to me. It was my own choices. Yes, the Lord was directing, but all of my past choices had produced this idol. I decided not to be angry with the collectors or even with their threats. I remained pleasant and thanked them for their call and wished them all a blessed day. I do not know how they felt, but I was doing fine. Who needs good credit anyway? Cash works great.

When mountains are removed and you are moving forward in obedience, it opens the door for the Lord to release His bounty. By August of 2012 Jan and I became completely debt free. We did have to settle on some credit cards, but we never missed a house payment or car payment and everything was paid off even the house and car. My credit idol was gone. It was so low that it did not register. It felt good to be free.

Our daughter had remarried and things for her began to level out. She and her husband found a good church, and slowly her walk with God became her own. Things began to change in her life, but she would still face some very difficult moments.

Another blessing was added in 2015 when Travis met Ruby, a beautiful Christian lady from the Philippians. She has a daughter the same age as Travis' daughter. In fact, the girls are only 4 months apart in age. Then in April, 2016 they were married, and I was given the honor of performing the wedding ceremony. We were joined by our daughter,

Hannah, and her husband, Adam. What a wonderful reunion! When the Lord moves, nothing is impossible. Nothing.

The Lord never promised an easy life, but He did promise a fruitful and abundant life. The fruitfulness and abundance will not look the same for everyone. This is why we need to keep vertical vision and not horizontal vision. What does the Lord have for each of us as families and individuals? Only He knows, but much of our journey will consist of facing mountain strongholds and the trees that grow from their soil.

We all have some of the same basic desires, and outwardly many will look the same. Only trusting the Lord can bring them to pass in His time. Life can be difficult at times, but as you learn to rest in Him, His peace that passes understanding will embrace you.

In His Time

As Hannah pressed into God for her own spiritual breakthroughs, we have seen God do a miracle in her life as well. She has the gift of discernment and encouragement. She speaks with love, but she is also very direct with what God's Word says. Many people seek her out for advice and encouragement from the Lord. Her time in the Word and in prayer has brought many breakthroughs in her life and the lives of others.

She and her husband desired to have children, but medical issues prevented it for many years. Then in 2014 Hannah began to bleed, and she was losing a lot of blood. She barely made it to the hospital before things turned deadly. She was pregnant, but it was an ectopic pregnancy, so she lost the baby. After the medical procedure she was told her chances of ever getting pregnant were pretty much nonexistent.

It is at these times in the valley of the shadow of death, when all your hopes and dreams are shattered, that the Shepherd of your life prepares a table before you in the presence of the enemy of your soul. Strangely enough He may not speak a word to you, but your spirit will whisper through the tears, "I will trust You."

What is happening is an uprooting of the mountain as it begins to tremble and loose its position. Laying down all your dreams and ambitions at the Lord's feet is the key. Speaking His word and allowing it to take root deep into your soul brings His strength and preparation for the journey. The choices made now will produce victory or defeat. God has a plan.

Then in September of 2017, Jan and I were at the store, Lowes to be exact, when we received a text and a sonogram picture of a tiny baby from our son-in-law, Adam. Yes, at age 40 Hannah was pregnant. You know, grandmothers squeal and get really excited even in public (granddads also, just more reserved). Grandmothers do not care. A baby is coming! So, in May of 2018 Amelia Grace came into the world, a very healthy and joyous little girl. And Nana says, "Virginia is not very close, you know," and she just looks at me, and I answered, "No, it is not."

New Blessings

It must be remembered that God does not only minster to us when everything is in order. It is a daily journey of walking and sometimes stumbling, but as we keep our eyes on the goal, His strength is made perfect in these earthen vessels.

The lesson learned here is to listen and speak only what God says. When the mountains of fear and doubt arise and you immediately run into God's presence, you will still see the mountain. However, you will see a much bigger God, and trusting in Him with shouts of "Grace, Grace" you will see God move on your behalf.

Travis, Ruby and the girls now live in Hawaii. Ruby has family there, and they are both blessed with tremendous paying jobs and a beautiful home. Then in July of 2019 they welcomed a baby boy, Keanu Daniel, into their lives, and Nana looks at Papa with that certain look and says, "Hawaii is a long way from Texas." What can I say, but? "Yes, it is, but Virginia is closer."

Fresh Insight

I am the type of person who learns best by repetition. Doing a task over and over with hands-on has always worked better for me. This is true with my reading and studying also. I will read things slowly on purpose. I will study the material over and over again until I come to an understanding or until it gets my thoughts on track to what God is saying. There was a time I would read through the Bible very quickly, and if I had what I thought was a basic understanding, I would move on. About fifteen years ago the Holy Spirit drastically changed that and put me on a new path of learning. One of reading very slowly and looking at every word and even the punctuation marks in the text. To my surprise this new study habit brought fresh insight and revelation to the text as I began to glean unknown depths to scripture previously passed over.

I also began an in-depth study on the "Power of Speaking Blessings" over my family and myself. As I began doing this consistently, it was the beginning of the removal of long, deep roots of failure from words spoken over me which had been passed down in my family.

Breaking Generational Curses

It is possible to break generational plantings and curses, but persistence and patience is required. Even words spoken in ignorance can be uprooted, but the key is listening to the Holy Spirit and walking in obedience and discipline. A seed puts down roots long before the plant breaks ground. It is drawing its strength from its source, whether good or bad. We need understanding to know how to fight these spiritual battles. Planting good seeds begins through confession and repentance. Our WORDS to each other and about each other play a huge part in breaking the curse. We must remember that we have the ability to create in people a life narrative of success or failure.

> Hosea 4:6
> *"⁶ My people are destroyed for lack of knowledge. Because you have rejected knowledge, I also will reject you from being priest for Me."*

Facing My Own Mountain Stronghold

I have told you some of my story and have shared several of the victories and difficult times our family has gone through, and I have spoken of the abiding presence of the Lord through them all. The grace of the Lord is truly amazing. His patience is unmatched, and He wants to fulfill His divine purpose in each of us.

What I now write is my own personal appointed time of deliverance from the spirit of fear. I will not go into detail on how it set up residence, but I can remember when it happened. Being five years old at the time, I was not aware of what had happened, but it put down very deep roots.

What I have learned on my journey is that the unseen realm or spirit world is far greater than we can imagine or have been taught, and its influence in our lives is ongoing. The adversary will allow you to have some breakthroughs from time to time, but he will keep a hook deep within you if he can. Spiritual clichés and titles mean nothing to darkness. It is not called warfare for nothing. We often think in simplistic terms when it comes to the influence and interaction the spiritual realm has with humanity. It is for this purpose Jesus gave Himself and gave specific instructions on facing strongholds and living in victory.

How the Lord brought me to my deliverance is evident in the things I have already said. The time had come for me to face this stronghold in my life once and for all, and the people Jesus prepared and placed in my life were a gift to me. I am eternally grateful for their ministry in my life.

I had been living in endless cycles of victories and defeats for many years, and the struggles were intense and overwhelming at times. In 2014 I came under such a heavy onslaught of darkness and depression that I thought I would die. I was led to call Dean and Carlene Truitt, retired missionaries who are dear friends. They had ministered at our church many times as well as to us when we were pastors. We arranged a time to meet with them. As they prayed and spoke with authority, I knew something had changed, but this was just the beginning. The mountain stronghold had been put on notice. Deliverance is coming, and all of Heaven is with it. You might ask, "Why did complete deliverance not happen then?" It must be noted that God has appointed days for His divine purpose to have the greatest impact. Remember, this is a journey to a specific destination, and everything had to be in order. However, the adversary would fight back.

In November, 2017 Jan and I visited New Hope Church in Abilene, Texas. We began to attend regularly and knew this was the place the Lord had for us at this time in our lives. We did not attend to get a platform to be known. It was and is a blessing to be in the services. Then in March of 2018 I was approached by Kathy Sanders, Pastor Chuck Farina's personal assistant. She said, "Pastor Chuck would like you to speak at one of the sessions during "Freedom Weekend." I was surprised at the offer and wanted more information about Freedom Weekend. She explained that the weekend is a time for people to encounter God in a fresh way to receive healing from past hurts and to bring restoration and freedom in areas of their lives. I was honored to be asked and told her, "Yes, I would love to participate." I then asked, "What is my topic?" Kathy said, "Living in Victory." As I pondered my subject, that cold dark voice began laughing, and my mind and emotions were gripped with fear. To make matters worse I was asked to turn in an outline and give a thirty-minute preview of my presentation. I would deliver the message to the pastor and the staff members beforehand so my timing and content could be evaluated.

I am not one to go back on my word, so as I prayed, my prayer was (1) Lord, help me not to bring a reproach to your name and (2) Please help me not make a fool of myself. The day came for my presentation to the pastor and staff, and fear gripped me so tight I felt sick and hardly slept the night before. I was asked to give a life experience with my subject matter. I chose to share about Talmadge's accident and how my family and I could live through this and not be destroyed.

Are you able to grasp this? I was battling a spirit of fear and failure, and my subject was on Living in Victory. Why was I so nervous? I had been in public ministry and preached for over 40 years and had never experienced such a debilitating fear. All I can say is that the time had come for this spirit of fear and failure to be completely uprooted, and it was coming in full force against me.

There was a staff meeting a few days before Freedom Weekend, and I asked Pastor Chuck why he asked me to speak? He said the Lord told him to have me speak on that subject. When God is bringing you to your destination, He is not setting you up for failure but victory even when victory is not in sight.

When the Sunday morning came to give my presentation, I was not as nervous as before, but I was still shaking and had to hold the mic with both hands next to my chest to keep it from shaking. After the session, during the break, many people came up to me and said how powerful the presentation was and what the Lord had spoken into their lives. Those in the fellowship who had prophetic insight came and said, "The Lord is preparing you for your future. Get ready." I was blessed to know Jesus was glorified, and I had survived.

What was happening? The Lord was letting me know that others had joined in the fight even though they were not aware of the war inside of me. WORDS MATTER!

The next February, 2019 Kathy approached me again and said, "Pastor Chuck wants to know if you will speak at another Freedom Weekend. Your subject will be the same –

Living in Victory. Would you be willing to teach on it again?" The importance of the **messenger** cannot be over stated, the words she delivered to me were just a question that needed an answer in the natural. But the power of those words was like a sword of the Spirit, and when I said yes, this time the fear and the mountain stronghold vanished. GONE, no thunder or flashes of light, no glory bumps, not anything. My enemy was GONE! Just like that, the question and my answer were all God wanted, and His victory became mine. Freedom is a marvelous gift, and if I may be so bold to say, Freedom Weekend was God's plan before time, and the topic, Living in Victory, was His plan for me.

The Lord was quick to give instructions on what I was to present this time. I was to mention the accident but to emphasize what He had revealed to me about TRUST. What He revealed is in the conclusion of this book.

I am eternally grateful to Pastor Chuck and his wife, Barb, for the confidence and graciousness they have extended. They have not only spoken into my life but Jan's also. Unknowing to them they have helped me to move off of the river bank into deeper waters. It is an honor to call them friends.

Planting Good Seeds

Many of the battles we fight can be avoided, if our **words** are directed by the Holy Spirit. You might say, "I did not know this." Take heart. God is the restorer of all that has been lost, and He will not disappoint you. Over the years we have planted many good seeds as well. We have seen those good seeds produce good fruit in our lives and the lives of our children. We have recounted some of them to you. Our Lord Jesus is so faithful.

While speaking at a local church one Sunday, I quoted Isaiah 54:17 and began sharing all the Lord has taught me regarding this portion of scripture. The Holy Spirit revealed that the verse was not just for me. He reminded me that I was the head of my family, and my spiritual authority and covering extended to my wife and each of my children and their respective families no matter where they lived. I could not go into their homes and dictate what they did. However, my wife and I can put a hedge of holy fire and protection around them. This is spirit. We may be living in the twenty-first century, but God's chain of authority is still in effect. Not only that, but after I am gone, what has been spoken will manifest in my future bloodline. With all of the darkness coming upon the world, if I have no other purpose in life, it will be to build a spiritual hedge of fire and protection around all my generations even if they never know my name. This is to the glory of God. Should the Lord tarry maybe many generations from now will come to know that their great, great, great granddad spoke blessings over them. I pray for my future generations, and I prophesy over them that they will come to know Him and be more than a conqueror in our Lord Jesus Christ. This is my God given authority. I can speak good things over myself and future generations.

Coming to this understanding should confirm the authority God has placed in your mouth. Instead of passing on burdens of fruitlessness and towering mountains, we can release a Holy Spirit filled army into future generations. Even if we are not remembered, our words and prayers will still reverberate around God's throne and all of heaven, and they will send terror and destruction on hellish forces.

I have spoken and written prophecies over each of our grandchildren. We FaceTime with our granddaughters when we can and speak blessings over them. We lift each one up daily before the Lord, and we speak his Name and His Word over them. We speak over our married children as well by standing on the authority of God's word. We believe that by speaking His word over them, we are planting good seeds in them. They need the covering of their parents even as adults. This is spirit, and distance is not a hindrance.

Jan and I are in one accord over each word spoken. We are confident that our bad plantings of the past are completely uprooted, and the good plantings from the Lord will continue to bring fruitfulness. It is in unity that God commands the blessing. Psalm 133.

Included at the end of this book are additional comments and testimonies by Hannah, Travis and Jan in their own words.

Chapter Eleven

Taking Your Inheritance

*A*re we there yet? We have spent much time talking about the journey and the destiny moments that bring us to our destination and inheritance. As our journey continues, we will see that not all trees and mountains are to be removed. The plantings of the Lord and the mountains of the Lord are to remain. This study has dwelt with Matthew 21:12-22 at the end of Jesus' ministry. It needs to be noted that Jesus began His ministry in the same way as recorded in John 2:13-19. In both places the scriptures state Jesus cleansed the Temple. The first time was near the beginning of His ministry and then finally a few days before His crucifixion. Both times were an illustration of His intended purpose to restore His original temple, mankind, to our place of dominion. We truly were "Created to be a Holy Habitation and More than a Conqueror."

> *Ephesians 2:1-7*
> *"And you He made alive, who were dead in trespasses and sins,*

² *in which you once walked according to the course of this world, according to the prince of the power of the air, the spirit who now works in the sons of disobedience,*
³ *among whom also we all once conducted ourselves in the lusts of our flesh, fulfilling the desires of the flesh and of the mind, and were by nature children of wrath, just as the others.*
⁴ *But God, who is rich in mercy, because of His great love with which He loved us,*
⁵ *even when we were dead in trespasses, made us alive together with Christ (by grace you have been saved),*
⁶ *and raised us up together, and made us sit together in the heavenly places in Christ Jesus,*
⁷ *that in the ages to come He might show the exceeding riches of His grace in His kindness toward us in Christ Jesus."*

Jesus is the beginning and the end, the foundation stone and the capstone. Only what is built on Him will stand. The scripture is full of references to the altars of God being rebuilt and proper worship being reinstated. No matter how long your altar has laid desolate and out of use, the Holy Spirit will reveal to the desperate soul the location of the altar. The Holy Spirit knows how to cultivate the plantings of the Lord and bring life and fruitfulness back into your barren life.

Job 14:7-9
"⁷ For there is hope for a tree, if it is cut down, that it will sprout again, and that its tender shoots will not cease.
⁸ *Though its root may grow old in the Earth, and its stump may die in the ground,*
⁹ *Yet at the scent of water it will bud and bring forth branches like a plant."*

Trust the Plan 185

We are so conditioned to see only darkness in any life or circumstance. So much so that words of life and encouragement are often ignored or scoffed at. But God has a plan for you, and His desire is for you to know it and live in it. Just as He spoke the creation into existence, we can speak His word in obedience to His command, and the results will be life-changing. Purpose today to begin speaking God's life-giving scriptures over yourself and your family. Your own life may seem dried up like dead dry bones, but God is calling you to speak in faith to those dry areas. You can speak His life into whatever is dead in your life just like He instructed Ezekiel.

> *Ezekiel 37:2-7*
> *"² Then He caused me to pass by them all around, and behold, there were very many in the open valley; and indeed, they were very dry.*
> *³ And He said to me, "Son of man, can these bones live?" So, I answered, "O Lord GOD, You know."*
> *⁴ Again He said to me, "Prophesy to these bones, and say to them, 'O dry bones, hear the word of the LORD!*
> *⁵ Thus says the Lord GOD to these bones: "Surely I will cause breath to enter into you, and you shall live.*
> *⁶ I will put sinews on you and bring flesh upon you, cover you with skin and put breath in you; and you shall live. Then you shall know that I am the LORD."'*
> *⁷ So I prophesied as I was commanded; and as I prophesied, there was a noise, and suddenly a rattling; and the bones came together, bone to bone."*

In this passage Ezekiel was told to speak the Word of the Lord to dead dry bones. Our words have authority and power when we speak God's commands. This is a process of spiritual growth and may require us to stop and take a closer look at a revealed truth in order for it to take root in our spirit. Time spent in prayer opens our heart to hear the Holy Spirit speak His truth and rebuild our life. Many times, we are in such a hurry to move on that we rush through our time in the Word. Bible reading plans are good, but do not get caught up in trying to read so fast that you miss the truth. Take time to hear God's voice through His Word. Ask the Holy Spirit to be your teacher and reveal His secrets to you. You just might find the Lord so close you can hear Him whisper your name.

We are often unprepared for what we will face each day, because we neglect quality time in God's Word and fellowship with His Spirit. Do not allow busyness or distractions to crowd these out. To do so can open a door for the adversary to replant his seeds. Remember, this is a lifetime journey. Hearing ears and seeing eyes are needed if you want to grow in faith and righteousness. They are essential to your worship and fruitfulness.

> *John 15:4-5*
> *"4 Abide in Me, and I in you. As the branch cannot bear fruit of itself, unless it abides in the vine, neither can you, unless you abide in Me.*
> *5 "I am the vine; you are the branches. He who abides in Me, and I in him, bears much fruit; for without Me you can do nothing."*

We were designed to be fruitful as we were created in the image of God. God created the heavens and the earth by His words, and we were given the authority over His creation. Even though that authority was subjugated by Satan, God can reverse it in our own lives. The first step to our own personal renewal is being born again and becoming a holy habitation full of God's Spirit and life. As we continue to submit ourselves to God's authority, in His name we have the power to take dominion over the powers of darkness and become more than a conqueror in Christ Jesus.

Minding our Words

The scripture tells us we speak out of the abundance of the heart. Matthew 12:34. This journey is designed to remove you from the kingdom of darkness and its controlling slave bondage mentality. We are told to renew our minds in Romans 12:1-2 and Philippians 2:5. Proper study and growth takes time as we learn how to test the spirits. I John 4:1. How will we recognize false narratives if we do not know what God has said in His Word?

> *2 Timothy 2:15-16*
> *"*^{15}*Be diligent to present yourself approved to God, a worker who does not need to be ashamed, rightly dividing the word of truth.*
> ^{16} *But shun profane and idle babblings, for they will increase to more ungodliness."*

Here Timothy is instructed to study to learn what is acceptable speech and what is vain. Words establish strongholds in our lives. We need to speak according to the Holy Spirit to pull down the strongholds of the adversary and to establish the Kingdom of God.

Sometimes a time of rest and healing is needed. This may look like a delay in our advancing, but these delays can be destiny moments for us. These are times to reflect on what God has already done and what He wants to solidify in our faith walk as we learn to trust Him. Occupying your promised inheritance requires trusting and living in God's love. His perfect love will always cast out fear, and you can rest assured He will bring His promise to completion.

I remember a time in Lubbock when the Lord gave specific instructions for me to leave my place of employment and wait on Him. I did so, and all was well for a season, but the test of waiting was not all that exciting. So, I decided to venture out on my own and look for work. Every door was closed. As I went to prayer, I complained about how things were turning out. Then the Lord asked me, "What was the last thing I instructed you to do on this matter?" I replied, "You told me to leave my job and wait on You, but that was six months ago." He said, "Have I told you anything different?" I said "No." He replied, "What I spoke to you still stands. Those are your instructions. When I am ready for you to do something different, I will tell you. Until then keep doing what I said."

From that experience I learned that the Lord does not continually repeat the same instructions every day. Small children need continued repetition, but as we mature and are trained and schooled in the things of God, instructions given once should be sufficient. Military commanders or employers do not repeat the same orders daily. We are in a spiritual war and are in the army of the Lord. Think of this. In the maturing process there is only one letter difference between the words **mature** and **manure**, and that is the letter "**t**", or if you please, the Cross. Daily trips to the altar of the cross at the mountain of the Lord brings us into maturity. Do not be in such a hurry. He sees the whole picture. We see only the moment we are in.

Isaiah 28:16
"ⁱ⁶ Therefore thus says the Lord GOD: "Behold, I lay in Zion a stone for a foundation, a tried stone, a precious cornerstone, a sure foundation; Whoever believes will not act hastily."

You may have been in a church service and heard a missionary or an evangelist give testimony after testimony of God's supernatural provision and healing, and they often recount the utter hopelessness of the situation. Yet, as they trusted the Lord for the need, they found His provision and help always there no matter how hard things were for them. In these moments we may think, "Wow! I would like to have that kind of testimony." Then a voice will whisper, "You can live like that. That is how you were created to live. Trust Me." It does, however, require us to step out in faith and speak God's Word over whatever emotion we may be feeling. This is our faith walk – meeting the test with obedience and trust.

Your Inheritance Awaits You

Do you know where you are? You have reached your destination. Your inheritance awaits you. You may say, "But wait. I am not perfect. I still have a pile of baggage." Here is the power of the grace and mercy of the Lord in your life. Remember, He is for you, not against you. If this is so, then who can stand against you? Romans 8:31. We are not invited to the Lord's table because we are baggage free. We are invited to come and be healed and be equipped for His Kingdom purposes and to receive our inheritance. If you are born of the Spirit of God, you are a child of God! Your greatest victories will be lived from your inheritance.

As the Israelites reached their destination and came face to face with Jericho, the mountain inside of them spoke to their unbelief, and fear kept them in bondage. As a result, many died in the wilderness. The land flowing with milk and honey is named "TRUST." And the entrance involves "Obedience." All they had to do was live God's way.

You are at your Jericho, the mountain. Your destination does not look like you thought it would, but your inheritance is there. This is your "day two" moment with Jesus saying, "You can curse that fruitless fig tree and speak to the mountain and cast it into the sea. And you hear, "Will you trust Me?"

Face to Face with Your Adversary

The war of words starts in your thoughts, and they are subtle and cunning. The tactic of the deceiver is actively working to redirect your eyes away from your destination into his snare with thoughts of, "Who do you think you are? Did God really say that to you?" He will challenge the very Word of God, every promise that has birthed hope, and every step of obedience that delivered you from Egypt. This journey has progressed from a FAITH walk to a TRUST walk. Who will you believe?

Jesus said SPEAK to the Mountain. The removal is not according to <u>what</u> we were, but WHO we <u>ARE</u> in HIM. He has cleansed you as His Temple. Now rise up and **BE** that Holy Habitation created for good works which God has already prepared for you from the very foundation of the world. Joshua went straight to the heart of the decision set before them.

Joshua 24:14-15
*"¹⁴ "Now therefore, **fear the LORD, serve Him in sincerity and in truth,** and put away the gods which your fathers served on the other side of the River and in Egypt. Serve the LORD!*
*¹⁵ And **if it seems evil to you to serve the LORD, choose for yourselves this day whom you will serve,** whether the gods which your fathers served that were on the other side of the River, or the gods of the Amorites, in whose land you dwell. But as for me and my house, we will serve the LORD."*
(emphasis mine)

The choice you make now will be your defining moment that releases LIFE to you and your household for generations to come, or it will reinforce the stronghold of the adversary over you and those generations. You may not be called to be a preacher or a speaker, but you do have a sphere of influence with people that no one else has. The Lord God has called you to be His imager, a reflector of His glory on Earth. We all have that calling. We need to be different than the world and to be someone who sows words of life in our family. We are complete in Him, and He wants to shine through us into our broken and incomplete world.

Chapter Twelve

Living In Your Inheritance

The Invitation. What you have been presented with is a very special invitation, an invitation to the Secret Place of the Most High.

Deuteronomy 29:29
"The secret things belong to the LORD our God, but those things which are revealed belong to us and to our children forever, that we may do all the words of this law."

The words the Lord planted in my spirit twenty years ago suddenly became crystal clear. We are all given a measure of FAITH, and that will produce HOPE. These come from the Lord. But TRUST is also a gift. It is **My Gift** back to Him. **Trust** is the connection to, not just knowing **about God,** but **knowing God.**

> *Psalm 91:1-2*
> *"He who dwells in the secret place of the Most High, shall abide under the shadow of the Almighty.*
> *² I will say of the LORD, He is my refuge and my fortress; My God, in Him I will trust."*

This was Paul's prayer in Philippians 3:10.

> *"That I may know Him in the power of His resurrection, and the fellowship of His sufferings, and being conformed to His death."*

This is the final step from moving away from being acquainted with His "acts" to living in His "ways." Psalm 103:7 says, *"He made known His ways to Moses, His acts to the children of Israel."*

This journey we are on and the destiny moments we face are designed to put to death the "slave bondage" mentality that has kept each of us from our destination and inheritance. Should not Jesus receive the reward of His suffering? - Our lives clothed in His righteousness and filled with fruits of righteousness which are by Christ Jesus to the glory and praise of God.

The Secret Place

It is a releasing of my will to His will. Your Kingdom come and Your will be done on Earth (me, as I am made of earth) as it is in heaven. When we do this, we suddenly find ourselves in the Secret Place of the Most High, and something AMAZING happens.

You know this is different, because HE WHISPERS YOUR NAME, and you almost become fearful. He Is Pure Holiness, Eternal Light and Life, the Almighty, the I Am Who I Am, the One Who Is, Who Was and Who Is to Come. This is my Creator, the One who LOVED ME before time.

Then you realize you feel something as He WHISPERS again. He is so close that you feel HIS BREATH. This is the BREATH that BREATHED life into Adam and gave him divine purpose. It is the same BREATH that JESUS BREATHED upon His disciples when He said, RECEIVE THE HOLY SPIRIT. It is the same BREATH given to us to empower us to fulfill our divine call and purpose for which we were originally created to live.

Then you realize there is more. HE is so close that you HEAR AND FEEL HIS HEART BEAT. He begins to reveal eternal truths to you that are not revealed to those who do not respond to His call. The truths He reveals in these moments were secrets, but once He reveals them to you, they now belong to you and your generations for eternity. As you remain in His presence, your INHERITANCE engulfs you. He gives you HIS REST.

Your Inheritance Is for Today

We may think that God's **rest** is for after this life has ended when we enter into eternity, but there is a rest that God promises you for everyday life. Because we are in a mortal body of flesh, we see our limitations, and much too often we still view ourselves through the things the deceiver says. Embrace this fact with the full assurance and backing of Christ's blood. For the believer our past is gone. The Lord does not see it anymore. He sees us as who we are in Him.

He sees us according to our future, and as we speak and live according to our future, it becomes our present. We are in this world but not part of it. Our lives should be a living testimony to the overcoming power of the Cross of Christ. He has filled us with His light. So, shine and proclaim liberty to the captives for the opening of blind eyes - both spiritually and physically. This is for you and your family. Take hold of it.

The world is a dark place. If the people of God are speaking and acting like the world, then where is the hope of our message? The world is crying out for a deliverer. Your family is crying out for a deliverer even if they do not realize it. That cry will be answered either by a false redeemer or the true redeemer. It is of the utmost importance we enter into our inheritance.

More Than A Conqueror

Receiving your inheritance and living as more than a conqueror here on earth will be found as you learn to trust your Savior. It is choosing to trust in your Heavenly Father through every part of your day and in every circumstance of your life. It is the assurance of His presence and care and peace and joy. It is resting in Him and allowing all of who He is to permeate your whole being no matter what you face in this life. It is allowing the Light and Glory of God to be evident in you and to flow through you. It is not always easy. It will take an act of your will to choose to walk in obedience and to trust Him with joy and without complaining.

> *Hebrews 4:10-11*
> *"ⁱ⁰ For he who has entered His rest has himself also ceased from his works as God did from His.*
> *¹¹ Let us therefore be diligent to enter that rest, lest anyone fall according to the same example of disobedience."*

Let me state it this way.

Trust leads to Obedience and
Obedience leads to the Secret Place and
The Secret Place leads to the Rest of God and
The Rest of God is your Inheritance,
The Armor of More than a Conqueror.

> *Psalm 37:3-7* (emphasis mine)
> *"³ **Trust** in the LORD, and do good;*
> ***Dwell** in the land, and feed on His faithfulness.*
> *⁴ **Delight** yourself also in the LORD,*
> *And He shall give you the desires of your heart.*
> *⁵ **Commit** your way to the LORD,*
> ***Trust** also in Him, and He shall bring it to pass.*
> *⁶ He shall bring forth your righteousness as the light,*
> *And your justice as the noonday.*
> *⁷ **Rest** in the LORD, and wait patiently for Him."*

> *Jeremiah 29:11*
> *"For I know the thoughts (plans and purposes) that I think toward you, says the LORD, thoughts (plans and purposes) of peace and not of evil, to give you a future and a hope."*

Will You Accept the Invitation?

Becoming a Holy Habitation and coming to your destination and inheritance very seldom resembles your imagination. There are many voices desiring to build their kingdom in your life for their own purposes. But we are called out to be different. We are called to be light and life in a dark world. We are called to seek the Lord. There will be things in this life that take us by surprise. Some may be painful, and some will be glorious. It is all part of the transformation and the journey. Embrace it and you will not be disappointed. The only one who can keep you from your destination and inheritance is you. If you are willing to embrace the journey, the Lord's strength is offered without measure. He has begun a good work in you, and He will bring it to completion on the day of Jesus Christ. Speak to your mountain with shouts of…

> Grace! Grace! Who Are You O' Great Mountain? I Am A Child of the Living God. I Have Been Bought with the Blood of Jesus Christ. And Not One, No Not One, Of Your Weapons Will Prosper Against Me nor My House. For My God Has Put You to an Open Shame. And the King of Kings and the Lord of Lords Has Crushed You Under My Feet!

So, Arise and Shine! The Glory of the Lord Is Upon You. Your Destination Is in Sight and Your Inheritance Is Sure!

TRUST THE PLAN

Additional

Testimonies

Hannah's Testimony

In Her Own Words

"This is the life of faith; for God will try the Truth of our Faith, so that the world will see that God has such servants as who will depend upon His bare Word." unknown.

Growing up in a Christian home, I was taught godly principles and attended church regularly. I accepted Jesus into my heart at a very young age, probably around five or six years old. I knew all the stories about Jesus. I acknowledged I was a sinner and wanted to go to heaven. I was baptized in my teen years and participated in the altar calls at church camp each summer. Each time I had an emotionally charged, religious experience. I shed tears and prayed and wanted to speak in tongues. Yet, my heart remained unchanged.

As I grew up, my life did not reflect the characteristics of a genuine follower of Christ. Yet, I considered myself to be a Christian. My walk was emotional and religious. It was not authentic. There is a difference between knowing about God and genuinely knowing God on a personal, intimate level. I had a desire to know God, but I did not fully understand what being a follower of Christ or being truly born again meant.

> *"Jesus said, 'Whoever desires to come after me, let him, 1) deny himself and 2) take up his cross and 3) follow me'."* Mark 8:34 NKJV

Here in Mark 8:34-38, Jesus marks the three non-negotiables of being His disciple. Guilt-free sin identifies your heart and your need for salvation.

I was married at 18 and left home a few months after graduating high school. I had a desire for God mainly because I wanted a good marriage and life – not because I had an interest in dying to self or serving the Lord with my life. I was even rebaptized in an emotional response to my brother's tragic accident resulting in his death.

After about 8 years my marriage had fallen apart. We both contributed to the breaking of the marriage through adulterous relationships and a lifestyle of partying. It was through this transition where the Lord began to lead me to a place of personal surrender to Him.

In a college psychology class, the professor asked us to write an essay on the role of women in marriage. Ironically, I was going through the divorce process while I was taking this class. I wrote about everything I had been taught from a biblical perspective on marriage and turned in my paper. At the next class the professor handed back my paper. He had given me a failing grade. Written in red across the front of the paper were the words, "I don't want to know what you were taught. I want to know what you think. You have a week to rewrite this paper."

At that moment I realized that I did not believe any of what I had written. I did not believe the Bible. I did not believe in God. I did not know what I truly believed. And, I realized that I did not care! I did not want to serve God or live for Him. I wanted to have fun and do my thing. So, that is just what I did!

Place of Surrender

Thankfully, although I was not saved, I did have a moral conscience, and there was some guilt over my behavior being morally wrong. I am thankful the Lord did not allow me to go so far as to have a seared conscience.

A year later the Lord allowed me to be brought to the end of myself, and in August of 2003 I came to a place of surrender to Jesus. This scripture began my journey.

> *"Trust in the Lord with all your heart, and lean not on your own understanding. In all your ways acknowledge Him, and He shall direct your paths." Proverbs 3:5-6 NKJV*

I was on my face in my apartment asking Him, "What does it mean to **trust** in You with all my heart? Show me how to trust in You alone." That day I made a willful decision to surrender my life, my mind, my will and my emotions to Jesus Christ, and I prayed, "I will trust in You, Jesus. Just show me how to walk it out. Show me how to live it." That was the moment I put my faith and my trust in the Lord Jesus. That was the moment He took out my heart of stone and gave me a heart of flesh. That day I stepped down off the throne of my heart and let the Lord have His rightful place as Lord of my life.

My lifestyle and desires instantly changed. For the first time in my life, I had a deep hunger for the Word of God. Reading the Bible literally sustained me, and I could not get enough of the Word. I actually enjoyed spending time in the

Word and in prayer. I also looked forward to going to church and being around other believers.

1 Peter 2:2 states we are to desire the Word of God like a newborn babe desires milk. One of the marks of a true believer is a hunger for the Word of God. Another mark is of a true believer is a change in lifestyle and desires.

Maturing in Christ

I am not going to say that I never struggled against sin again. The process of sanctification is difficult and long. Backsliding and doubting His Word are real dangers. I have experienced firsthand the shame of denying Him through my choices and actions, regrettably, more than once.

Even in those moments of weakness, when fear or doubt or the stubbornness of the flesh rises up, there is a battle for who will have the victory. Will I let Jesus stay on the throne of my heart? Some of those battles have had great casualties and have not been won quickly. Those willful struggles are not worth the pain and consequences either. It is best to "trust and obey for there is no other way to be happy in Jesus" as the song goes.

By His grace, the Lord led me to a small church, Calvary Chapel, where Pastors Mike and Sue were willing to challenge me and to speak the hard but necessary truths into my life. They labored tirelessly to help bring me to a place where I could mature in Christ. Many times, Pastor Mike would say, "If you are a Christian, why are you not acting like it?" Or he would say, "Your behavior follows your beliefs. What you really believe will come out in your actions."

At any moment, I can make a willful choice to turn away. Jesus said that He does not have any pleasure in one who puts his hand to the plow and then turns away. We cannot lose our salvation, but we can certainly give it back. His word in Hebrews exhorts us to hold fast and not drift away. Our hearts are deceitfully wicked.

Hebrews 3:12-19 warns us to be aware of a heart of unbelief, sinful desires and rebellion. The parable of the sower in Matthew 13:1-13, Luke 8:4-15 and Mark 4:1-20 exhorts us to continually prepare our hearts as good ground for the Word to grow. We must guard against having stony ground in our hearts and allowing the birds (the enemy) to snatch away the seeds of His Word.

The Bible says we overcome by the blood of the Lamb and the word of our testimony, Revelation 12:11. What I have shared is only a snapshot of the work of His grace in my life. It is only the beginning of many lessons the Lord has taught me. The first step is always the surrendering of our will. The next step is taking up our cross and the third, following Jesus. Repentance is a lifestyle. Sanctification is a lifelong process.

Over the years there have been many opportunities to be tested. The moment I feel confident that I have arrived spiritually, another test comes to exhort me to put no confidence in the flesh but in the power of God.

The Test of Waiting

One test began a few years after I was remarried when Adam and I would face the struggle of infertility. This season of waiting and trusting was very difficult. I knew having a child would not happen because of my own strength. It would be a work of the Lord, not a work of the flesh. I would say, "Lord, Sarah was 80, and yet You worked in that seemingly impossible situation." I was learning to lean on the Lord more fully and to not walk in my own confidence. My responsibility was to be faithful to what He said to do in His Word.

Our journey started in 2010 when we began trying to have children. After two unsuccessful years we sought fertility treatment which led to surgeries all of which were ultimately unfruitful.

Then on April 13, 2013 the Lord gave me the promise in His Word found in Psalms 113:9.

> *"He makes the barren woman to be a homemaker and mother of children. Praise the Lord!" Amplified*

He spoke so clearly to my spirit. This was His plan and purpose for me personally. Yet, His promise was not fulfilled right away. It would take time, and it would build my faith as I learned to stand solely on His Word. I would have to look at all things through the eyes of faith, not at my circumstances. Nor could I trust my feelings. It was a time of learning to love Jesus <u>more</u> than my feelings and a time of choosing to do what was right, even if I did not feel like it.

One of my favorite quotes by the late Pastor Chuck Smith is:

> *"You won't find the solution to your problems by looking at yourself or by looking at others. Direct your thoughts away from the problem and put them on God, away from your own weakness and onto His strength. You need to remember that God loves you and is in control of the circumstances that surround your life."*

Did I truly believe God was in control of all the circumstances in my life? If so, then I needed to act like it!

Test of Trust

In February of 2014 I began experiencing a sharp pain in my lower back and abdomen. It went on for about three days, and I felt horrible. On a Friday I left work and drove myself to the Urgent Care Clinic. While at the clinic, I passed out briefly in the bathroom. Convinced I had a kidney stone, I was shocked to learn I was pregnant. The joy was short lived, because the pregnancy was ectopic, and there was a concern my fallopian tube would rupture.

My husband drove me to the hospital 45 minutes away. By the time we arrived at the hospital, I could barely stand up. While doing an ultrasound, they discovered my body cavity was full of blood because my tube had burst, and I was bleeding internally. The doctor immediately prepared me for emergency surgery. They estimated I had lost 1/3 of my blood volume. By the hand of the Lord and His grace I made it through the surgery. The baby did not make it.

I was determined to trust the Word that the Lord had given me. I refused to allow myself to doubt. I would ask the Lord when and how He would accomplish His plans, but I would not allow myself to have unbelief. One of the promises of His Word that I clung to during this season of waiting is Romans 15:13.

> *"May the God of my hope so fill me with all joy and peace in believing through faith that by the power of the Holy Spirit, I will abound and overflow with hope and confidence in His promises." Romans 15:13 Amplified*

I had to make a deliberate choice to Hope in His Word, Trust His Promises and Walk with Joy. Gregg Laurie describes HOPE like this: "Holding on with Patient Expectation."

The Promise Fulfilled

Then on September 10, 2017, four and one-half years after the word and promise from the Lord, I took a pregnancy test, and it was positive. I literally laughed with **joy**. I knew the Lord had fulfilled His promise to me.

On May 15, 2018, (a week late, mind you) we welcomed Amelia Grace into our arms. Her name, Amelia, in Hebrew means "a work of the Lord," and Grace means "His unmerited favor." Her name stands as a testament to God's promise and His unmerited favor in our lives.

God kept His promise to me, and it is my testimony of His unfailing love and faithfulness. Even when I have made mistakes, doubted and been unfaithful, His grace and mercy has endured. It is only by His grace that I am saved. One of my favorite verses is found in Job 23:10.

> *"But He knows the way that I take; when He has tested me, I will come forth as gold." Job 23:10 NKJV*

Travis' Testimony

In His Own Words

In order to give some perspective, I feel compelled to fill in the gap regarding my conversion experience and who I was before that day. It should be understood that, obviously, I was raised under the instructions of the Bible. I had gone to church and private Christian schools most of my younger life, so I was versed in the scriptures and was baptized more than once. I had "confessed with my mouth" that Jesus was Lord and that he died for my sins and rose again. All of this was in my understanding, so I lived my life believing I was a born-again Christian. I believed that if I were to die, I would go to heaven. But I did not "walk the walk" so to speak. I lived my life as I chose in sin and in debauchery. I will not entertain you with my old life beyond that I lived like the old cliché, "Pastors' kids are always the worst." I often laughed as I tried to live up to those words. That is until January 7th, 2008, the date of my salvation.

This part of my story begins in Abilene, Texas in the fall of 2007. I was sitting on a Harley Davidson motorcycle in the parking lot of Hope Chapel (Hope 4 Life) Church when the dominoes of my life began to fall. I had a cigarette in my hand

and a bandana on my head. The image I was trying to convey was that of a rough biker type. However, in truth, I was a weak-willed person who loved his sin and wanted to stay in it. The pastor of the church at that time was Scott Hassett. This man of God became the single, most beloved man in my life, save my father. The man whom God would use to turn this stubborn man around and lead him to the cross.

Scott was chatting with me about my newborn daughter whom I had not yet seen. We were chatting about my life, and I told him I was thinking about coming to church again. I distinctly remember him telling me to come or not, but do not act like you are interested when you are not. I flicked my cigarette to the ground, and Scott was not happy. He told me to pick it up, that he didn't appreciate me disrespecting the church grounds. When I laughed, he told me that if I did not pick it up, I would not be welcome there. I was a little taken back by this young new pastor who was not playing the nice pastor game I was used to. He was supposed to grovel and to invite people, not tell a person they would not be welcome. I picked up the cigarette butt. Scott went on to tell me that I was not really serious about this whole church thing. He told me I only wanted God to fix my problems, so I could go on living my life like I wanted. He was not nice at all in the face of my sin. He was blunt when I was accustomed to "sweeter talk" - the kind of talk that makes you feel good - the kind of talk that comforts you and allows you to go on sinning while getting an emotional high.

In that moment I began to hold him in great respect. He did not sugarcoat the truth. Today, as I sit writing this out, I am emotional about Pastor Scott. I will always love that man like a brother. He was and always will be my best friend. He was, in fact, the man God used to tip the first domino in my life which would ultimately lead to my death and rebirth in Christ Jesus.

Fast-Forward to January, 2008

I will leave out the details of my life of sin. I hate it, and I am ashamed of it. It is for this reason I skip ahead to the night of my new birth. I will offer this though. I had celebrated New Year's Eve with friends. The next day I received a phone call from them and was told I wasn't welcome anymore. Things had gotten out of hand during the celebration, and they wanted to cut ties for a good long while. I was crushed and had nowhere to turn. With no friends to hang out with, there was nothing between me and my obvious failure of a life. I spent the next few days desperately searching for a way to fix the mistakes that had led me to this crossroads in my life.

January 7th, 2008
The Date of My Salvation

I was in a state of sadness that I had never experienced before. I was friendless and feeling alone and facing a child custody battle for my daughter that seemed an impossible task. I had nowhere to turn. I ended up looking to my parents for guidance that night.

My father was at work as I recall, and I found my mother in her room quietly reading her Bible. I sat down and began to tell her about the events that had taken place. I asked her to pray and ask God to help me. My mother listened. She quietly took in the words of her son and finally responded. She said, "Travis, I can pray for you, but you also have to pray for yourself."

What follows is my account of an encounter with God that changed my life forever. I will never doubt there is a holy God, and He deserves my life in its entirety. My mother began to pray, and as I remember, it was short. She simply said, "Lord, Travis would like to talk to you. He needs you. Will you please hear him?" I remember thinking, "What a short prayer." It was my turn, so I bowed my head and began my prayer much like I had many times before. "Heavenly Father, I want to ask for your help. I want to ask you to..."

Standing Before a Holy God

In an instant I was not in my mother's room but in a different place. I distinctly remember a hand grabbing me by the throat and slamming me to a wall. Then there was a voice so thundering and so loud that words cannot describe it. This roaring voice was directly in my face and yet thundering all around from every direction. It said, "HOW DARE YOU COME INTO MY PRESENCE AND ASK FOR MY HELP! LOOK AT YOUR LIFE!"

Then my entire life was laid out in front of me. Every sin, every cuss word, everything I had ever done in secret. EVERYTHING. I tried to interject and to make excuses, but each time the holiness of God slapped any excuse away. GUILTY! I tried again and again to explain. GUILTY! Every time I had the chance to do right and didn't - GUILTY! Every time I took His name in vain - GUILTY! Every time I could have truly repented and did not - GUILTY! Every despicable sin and every thought and action was laid out. Every time there was a sin presented, I was also shown the opportunity given not to follow through with that sin, but I sinned anyway. Every tiny detail of my life - the sin and insult of it all. GUILTY! GUILTY! GUILTY! I was filled with the knowledge of all my sin and its implications. I was aware of all my guilt and what it meant for me. I was made to see my life through God's eyes, and I saw the absolute insult I was to His holiness. I knew. I KNEW what I had done and what I deserved.

When it was done, I was weeping harder than I knew possible. I knew the holiness of God, the righteousness of God, the wisdom of His requirements, and the justice of His wrath. I deserved hell. I deserved an eternity of damnation and more for my insult against His Deity. I was worse than filth. I did not need to be thrown into the pit of fire by someone else. I was willing to cast myself into the pit, simply because HE was worthy to be loved and obeyed, and I DESERVED it. I wept with the deepest of sorrow and understood the scripture that says...

> *"But the sons of the kingdom will be cast into the outer darkness, where there will be weeping and gnashing of teeth." Matthew 8:12 NKJV*

The Sacrifice

That's when something happened. I looked up and saw that I was in a large room. This room was shining like the sun with gold and white from every conceivable direction. I saw a large white throne that also shone with the same brightness but somehow stood out from the blinding light all around. On the throne was someone whose appearance was so bright I couldn't make out the features of the one sitting there. A great fear was upon me, and I knew I was in the presence of a Holy God. But still, I did not comprehend what was happening.

Then I saw from behind the throne another who was like the one sitting. One whose clothes were shining like the sun and whose face was shining brighter than any white I had ever seen. He said no words, but the feeling I felt at His presence was different - not so frightening. He approached me, and I knew He was offering me something, though I did not know what it was. I only knew that what He offered would make all my guilt go away. I tried to decline because of the guilt I was feeling. My shame was so great, and I knew I didn't deserve what was being offered. But just like the excuses I had made for my sin, this too was thrown aside, and it was presented again. I remember accepting, or perhaps a better understanding would be to say, I submitted. Instantaneously, a white-hot bar of solid fire hit me in the chest. It took my breath away. It's difficult to explain what this felt like, but it seemed as if I was being burned or seared or perhaps scoured raw inside. It hurt yet brought relief at the same time.

The next thing I remember is I was back in my mother's room blubbering like a baby and sweating all over. I knew I had just had an encounter with a Holy God, but I did not comprehend what had just happened. As I stated before, I had been raised in a Christian home and believed I was already born again. It took me a few days to conclude that before that day, I was not born again. Before that day, had I died, I would have spent eternity in hell. I understood that the One whom I had seen on the throne was God the Father, and the One who had taken my guilt was Jesus. I remember saying to Scott, "I think I just got saved."

Delivered

Once I understood that I had truly been born again, things began to change in my life. I was instantly delivered from alcohol and did not want to drink anymore. But I still had many other bad habits to work on. This was when Scott Hassett and I began an amazing journey in which I would be pressed and tested. I began to understand the scripture that says.

> *"Therefore, my beloved, as you have always obeyed, so now, not only as in my presence but much more in my*

absence, work out your own salvation with fear and trembling." Philippians 2:12 NKJV

I recall one occasion when I was challenged by Pastor Scott to quit smoking. Actually, as I remember it, he pulled a "fast one" on me while we were chatting one afternoon in his office. I was telling him that I really wanted to quit smoking for my daughter, because I didn't want her to grow up around it. I felt God was telling me that I had two paths in front of me. One in which I smoked and the other in which I did not smoke. I felt God was telling me He had many blessings in store for me if I would drop that nasty habit, but I wanted door number two. So, like any good pastor, Scott suggested we pray. I acquiesced, and he led me in prayer. As we prayed, he encouraged me to promise God that I would not smoke from that day forward. I did, and when we were done, he held out a trash can. You, sly fox!

Scott: You promised God you wouldn't smoke anymore, so toss 'um.
Me: HAHA, seriously bro?! I just bought this pack.
Scott: You made a promise to God. Are you going to keep it or break it?

I tossed the brand-new pack into the rubbish and started my journey to being smoke free. It was not easy, but with Christ in me who could be against me? I struggled for a long time but finally won out. But it didn't end there. I loved smoking. It was a pass time, and I missed it. Eventually, I started smoking again, and I felt it impossible to quit after that. Until one day while I was alone and praying, I had had enough. I stood up and rebuked the addiction in the name of Jesus! I crushed the almost new pack of cigarettes and threw them in the rubbish. Then I grabbed my chest and said, "I'm done with this addiction, Satan! I'm finished with allowing you to keep me in this unhealthy state!" And I flung my hand out as if to rip the addiction out of my chest, and I cast it away... It worked! I quit cold turkey that night and have not had one craving for a smoke ever since. In fact, the smell of cigarettes makes me nauseous to this day. What a wonderful God we serve. He delivered me from that addiction once and for all!

God Has Your Back

This was not the only time I experienced God's power. There was a time when I was feeling very ill in my stomach. During those years I was often stricken with debilitating stomach cramps. I had gone to the doctor and been examined, but there was not much he could do. I most likely had developed ulcers after getting food poisoning from fish. If I ate the wrong thing, it made me very sick. I was at work, and while I wanted to go home, I needed the money, so I just pushed through the day.

One of my co-workers was making fun of me and hazing me. No big deal on normal days as we all have to have thick skin in the real world. But on this particular day I was not in the mood. As he ramped up his teasing, I became aggravated at him and said, "Ok dude, if you think you can handle this better than me, then you can have it" I grabbed my stomach as if to grab the sickness, and as I walked by I slapped him on his stomach saying, "Here, it's yours. I don't want it anymore."

About 10 minutes later I noticed that I was beginning to feel a lot better. I didn't put the pieces together until I saw my co-worker clutching his stomach. He looked at me with a bewildered look, and I started to put the pieces together and wondered what had just happened. He got so sick that he hurled in the trash can and had to go home. He never again hazed me when I was feeling ill, but then again, I never again felt ill to my stomach after that day. I'll leave it there for you to ponder, but as for me, I believe that God was backing me up that day.

Pride Got in the Way

As I have tried to walk the narrow road of righteousness, I will not lie to you and say that I did not fail. In fact, I failed in the most spectacular ways imaginable. The first few years were years of great growth and love for Jesus and what He had done for me. It was a time when my favorite scripture came to life for me.

> *"I have been crucified with Christ. It is no longer I who live, but Christ who lives in me. And the life I now live in the flesh I live by faith in the Son of God, who loved me and gave himself for me."* Galatians 2:20 NKJV

I have failed so many times in my walk with Jesus. But I have learned that just because you fail does not mean you give up. It just means you have learned a new way not to follow Jesus. When I was young in the Lord, I began to see myself as very pious. I believed that those around me were destined for hell if they didn't live the pious life I did and that any failure was unacceptable. I erroneously believed that if you had not had the same kind of experience I did, then you were never truly saved. I was puffed up on my own righteousness. It didn't take long before God allowed me to be humbled. I was brought very low and made to understand the mercy and grace of God in a much deeper way.

Even now I pray daily and thank Jesus for His tender mercy and grace in my life. I have failed Him so many times. I will never forget my ups and down in Jesus. It was through those trials that my faith in Him was, to a point, perfected. Yet, I have so much further to go.

I have learned that even in failure there is a love that transcends any other we can ever understand. While His love and mercy are sometimes overlooked, it is ever-present in my life. I often relate my life to that of Peter who denied Christ three times. I am comforted knowing that even those who walked with Jesus were capable of failing him and knowing that even after this, Jesus came to Peter and forgave him. One of my favorite stories in the Bible is the parable of the prodigal son in Luke 15:11-32. In this story I am most touched by verses 17-20.

> "17 "When he came to his senses, he said, 'How many of my father's hired servants have food to spare, and here I am starving to death!
> 18 I will set out and go back to my father and say to him: Father, I have sinned against heaven and against you.
> 19 I am no longer worthy to be called your son; make me like one of your hired servants.'
> 20 So he got up and went to his father. "But while he was still a long way off, his father saw him and was filled with compassion for him; he ran to his son, threw his arms around him and kissed him." NKJV

During my failures God did not turn his back on me but waited and allowed me to fail and learn. He allowed me to gain some of the wisdom of His ways. And when I came to my senses I returned to the Lord. But while I was a long way off, He came running! He swept me up in His arms and loved me as if I had never left. He forgave me and clothed me.

Then He blessed me with a wife and family. When I wanted to move to Hawaii, He made a way where there seemed to be no way. I still say to Him, "Lord, I am not worthy of the blessings and mercy you continuously pour out on my life." He continues to bless me in spite of my many failures. I now live my life like I never dreamed I would be able. The sun and sand of Hawaii are a testament to God and the wonders of His creation. Each weekend is like a vacation, and my toes seem to always have sand between them, and my pocket always holds a seashell. I AM BLESSED.

Now, lest anyone think it was by my own hard work that I have attained this, I will say this so you know it once and for all. I am nothing without Jesus Christ the Son of the living God. It is because of His will that I am beside still waters. I can do nothing without Jesus, but I can do all things through Christ who strengthens me. Philippians: 4:13

I write this last portion to express a great concern that has haunted me ever since the night of my salvation experience. I was raised believing in the Bible. I truly believed I was saved. I had followed the instructions that said all I needed to do was to confess with my mouth and believe that Christ was the Son of God, but if I had perished before that day, I would be in hell. How many others have been raised under the teachings of the Bible and yet are not saved?? How many will say on the last day, LORD, LORD... but be cast into the lake of fire? How many will perish believing they will be in heaven and instead find out they have another destination?? How many?

Jan's Testimony

In Her Own Words

One aspect of my husband's book has been about learning to trust God's plan during difficult circumstances. When this project began, I had no idea it would include stories told by other members of the family. My sister asked if I was going to share my side of things. I just sat there unable to answer as the thought of putting emotions on paper seemed overwhelming and brought a kind of panic. It was hard enough reading my husband's words on the subject.

Then I told our Lord that if He wanted me to say something I would do so, but He would have to help me and tell me what to share. As I submitted to the Lord, I knew this was not about me. It is about the next generation and whoever else might need my perspective to get through a tough day.

The Prayer Meeting

The night Travis and I went to prayer in my bedroom was the most intense and precious prayer time I have ever had with anyone, and I have been in a lot of prayer meetings. Before he wrote his portion to be included in his dad's book, I knew nothing of what happened to him that night. What he described is accurate except that I did not know what was going on inside of him. I only knew he was truly broken before God.

At first, he started praying calmly, but then things took a sudden turn, and he began to weep uncontrollably. I remember him saying things like, "You don't understand what I've done. I don't deserve to be forgiven." I thought he was speaking to me. As he continued to sob, I was broken and wept as I prayed. What I remember is this. He prayed; then I prayed; then he prayed again; then I prayed. It was intense. I now know why. I had no idea he was having his own Damascus Road God encounter. I only knew I saw a broken young man, and as I wept, I interceded for my son.

When we finished praying, I noted the time. We had been praying for 45 minutes. I came away saying, "Lord, you said a broken and contrite heart You would not turn away." I held my breath for the next few days. Was this real, or would it be like all the other times before? Let me tell you. It was real. There was a change, a definite change in Travis, and everything began to fall in place for him after that.

Most people do not have such a dramatic salvation experience. I believe that because of Travis' strong personality and stubborn ways, it was the only way the Father could get his attention. I am so glad He did, and I praise Jesus for saving my son.

My Own Salvation Testimony

As for my own salvation experience, I was saved at age 8. It was a Sunday morning at the Dallas/Oak Cliff Foursquare Church. I remember it well. Pastor Faulkner gave an altar call after his message, and I responded. I was the only one who went forward. It was quite a large church, and we were sitting in the middle of a long row. Without any hesitation I stood up and made my way over the people. The pastor came down from the pulpit and prayed with me. It was as simple as that.

At age 11 on a Sunday night service in an Assembly of God Church in Greenville, Texas, I was filled with the Holy Spirit and spoke in other tongues. Then at age 13 I was refilled with the Holy Spirit at a Foursquare summer camp in Siloam Springs, Arkansas. Later that week I was baptized in the camp swimming pool.

After high school graduation I knew I wanted to serve the Lord any way I could, but I did not know in what way. I only knew that whatever I chose to do, it had to be with the same dedication. I went to L.I.F.E. Bible College that fall. I have often wondered if I was actually called into the ministry as I cannot say that I had a specific call. During my teen years I had much admiration for the different men of God who spoke at church camp. I remember saying to myself or maybe it was to the Lord, "I want to marry a man like that." God granted me that desire, and I have come to understand that perhaps He called me to be a pastor's wife.

What this tells me is that we all need to be in church services where the Word of God is preached as it gives opportunity for the Holy Spirit to deal with our hearts. These are seeds planted in our spirit, and God's Word will never return void.

My children had to find God in their own way, and it took them going through some difficult trials. When they did surrender to the Lord, they already had a good foundation under them. True is the promise, *"Train up a child in the way he should go, and when he is old, he will not depart from it."* Proverbs 22:6. There were many verses I clung to while my children were afar off from the Lord. There were days of great travail and warring in the spirit for their souls.

I believe what we experience in the Lord as a child is real. It is the Holy Spirit drawing us to Jesus even if it is not completely understood. These are destiny moments. However, when we become adults, we have to decide if we will continue in our childhood faith or walk the way of the world. We all have to come face to face with our own sin and our own need of the Savior. There have been times when my Christian walk was carnal and selfish mainly because I neglected spending personal time in prayer and in the Word.

My Trust Walk

Since our church had a small Christian school, I spent every day with my sons and was their teacher on many subjects. Often, I would have to hide a giggle as I watched Talmadge's eyes follow that "special" girl across the room. It is a sweet memory. On Sundays at the piano, I would have to remind him not to hit me in the back of the head with his guitar as he stood behind me looking over my shoulder at the music.

Some of the letters we received were from girls Talmadge knew from summer camp. One by one they told us of how much Talmadge meant to them, and several even told us of a cheap, plastic ring he had given them. What? He had purchased several twenty-five cent rings out of a gumball machine and given one to each girl. They thought it was so sweet, and some still had theirs. Ha! Such a Casanova. Well, I guess if you are only 16 that is all you can afford. Silly boy. Memories do grow sweeter, and they don't hurt so bad anymore.

I won't even try to touch on the subject of grief. What I will talk about is some of the things that helped me personally get through those first few years after Talmadge's homegoing. It truly was about everyday trust.

Young people are so open. When I came back to work after the funeral, I could tell the students were nervous. They were worried about saying too much to me for fear of making me cry. Adults are too fearful about such things. I know I was. You want to say you are sorry but are fearful it will upset the person. Hey, can I tell you? It is ok to cry. I told them that I might start crying one day, but if that happens just stand up and put your arms around me. That is all I need. The day did come when sorrow overwhelmed my heart, and I started to tremble. It was our sweet Katie who jumped up and put her arms around me. That was all it took. We stood there a minute; then we both took a deep breath and were able to go on with the day. That moment is precious to me.

The first thing I told the students was I did not want them to be afraid to talk about Talmadge. They could talk to me about him. In fact, I wanted them to, and I asked them to write me a memory. So, for the next six months, we all began working through this loss in very tangible ways. I put all their memories, stories, poems and songs into a booklet and made copies for everyone and even took copies to church camp the next summer.

The school always participated in a year-end school convention where the students entered a variety of contests. One thing we put together was a "James Dobson" style radio program titled, *How to Deal with the Death of a Friend*. One student was the interviewer and asked questions of the others. We all cried through those recordings. It did not win at convention, but it had the judges in tears. This was me helping them work through their grief, but it was therapy for us all.

Often, I cried all the way to work and would have to compose myself before going in to school. Then a student would be having a bad day, and I would say to them all the things I knew to be true in my spirit even though every fiber of my being was screaming out something else. By the time I had encouraged them, I had encouraged myself. It is times like these when your faith walk becomes a trust walk.

This was all in that first year. You see, I was very much aware of this. As a teacher in a Christian school, I was trying to teach them how we live life with Jesus as our focus, but I also felt very acutely that I needed to show them how a believer should walk through death. All of us were deeply affected and profoundly changed by what we had experienced together. It is a moment in time that is forever locked into our memories, and we are knitted together in a bond I think only we understand.

Then came year two. And for those who have walked through grief, you know it does not end in a year or even two. Many more years of missing are ahead of you, and it won't be completely over until you are all together again. The students moved on with life as people do. But our family was still in deep turmoil. I knew I would not be ok until my children were ok, and that would take many more years.

So how do you move on? How do you get through the nights? How do you silence the taunts of the accuser? For me it was putting scripture to memory. I memorized large portions of scripture – whole chapters at a time and would have people at church test me on them to make sure I knew them. When night came, I would review them over and over again in my head until I fell asleep. In doing this I was able to drown out the "other voices" for a while. You may feel you cannot do that, but there are other ways to get through those dark seasons. I have also used my YouTube app to play scripture readings or music at night. The key is to never allow the darkness to define our God. Hang on even when you don't understand. Things will and do get better over time.

Talmadge is not lost to me. I know exactly where he is. He is with Jesus, and if Jesus is in my heart, then Talmadge cannot be very far away, can he?

This too is a lifelong journey of learning to trust and choosing to trust in spite of conflicting emotions. I know in whom I have believed, and I am persuaded that He is able to keep that which I have committed to Him. My faith is rooted in the unshakeable truth of our Savior's death and resurrection. My hope is grounded in His promise that He will return for His own. Since my past is forgiven and my future is secure, I can trust Him for today. I trust the plan.

Prayer of Repentance and Dedication

Holy Spirit, thank you for revealing to me that I need a Savior. I confess that I have chosen to remain in the kingdom of darkness for far too long. But I long to be free. I confess I am a sinner, and Jesus died and rose again to make me His Holy Habitation. Thank you for His cleansing blood that brings me into God's Kingdom of Light.

Today, I choose to make You the Lord of my life. I renounce and turn from my sin to the Living God. I will follow You all the days of my life. Because of what Jesus did for me, all my darkness is gone, and I am a new creation. I am complete in Him, and His Glory now fills me with His Life and Light.

Thank you for opening my eyes to the destination and inheritance that is mine in Christ Jesus, and thank you for making it possible for me to become "More than a Conqueror."

Blessings and Declarations

There is power in the spoken word. You can speak God's Word over yourself and your family. These are a few scriptures we have endeavored to speak daily.

Deuteronomy 29:29
The secret things belong to the Lord our God, but those things which are revealed belong to us and to our children forever that we may do all the words of this law.

Isaiah 54:17
No weapon formed against you (me) shall prosper, and every tongue which rises against you (me) in judgment you (I) shall condemn. This is the heritage of the servants of the Lord, and their righteousness is from ME, says the Lord.

Today, I choose to walk in the provision of the Cross and the power of Jesus' resurrection for I was created to be a Holy Habitation for the presence of the Living God.

I bring every thought and word into obedience with the Word of God. I purpose to speak blessings and not curses over myself and my family. God is the God of the impossible and will do the impossible IN me, THROUGH me and FOR me.

Hebrews 13:20-21
Now may the God of peace who brought up our Lord Jesus from the dead, that great Shepherd of the sheep, through the blood of the everlasting covenant, make you (me) complete in every good work to do His will, working in you (me) what is well pleasing in His sight, through Jesus Christ to who be glory forever and ever.

End Notes

Chapter 2: The Journey Begins
1. Charles (Chuck) Missler, PH. D: *I Jesus, An Autobiography*, pages 114 &117, Koinonia Institute.
2. Paris Reidhead: From a recorded message entitled "Ten Shekels and a Shirt."

Chapter 3: Purpose of Creation
3. Dr. Michael Heiser; *The Unseen Realm* pages 46-47, Lexham Press
4. Note from *Strong's Concordance,* #H3335
5. Note from *Strong's Concordance,* #H5301
6. Arthur W. Pink: *Exposition of the Gospel of John* page 1100, Bottom of the Hill Publishing
7. Dr. Michael Heiser: *The Unseen Realm*, page 40-43, Lexham Press

Chapter 4: God's Mandate
8. Note from *Strong's Concordance,* #H8104
9. Note from *Strong's Concordance,* #H4390
10. Dr. Michael Heiser, *The Unseen Realm*, Chapter 11, page 87, Lexham Press
11. Note from *Strong's Concordance* #H7287
12. Note from *Strong's Concordance,* #H6191

Chapter 5: Lost Inheritance
13. Dr. Michael Lake: *The Shinar Directive*, pages 38-40, Defender Publishing

Chapter 6: Deliverance from Bondage
14. Note from *The Genesis Hebrew-Chaldee Lexicon*
15. Chart from *Zondervanacademic.com*

16. Note from *Strong's Concordance* #H6031
17. Definition from *Webster's New World College Dictionary*

Chapter 7: Cleansing the Temple
18. Note from *Strong's Concordance*, #G4137

Chapter 8: Cursing the Fig Tree
19. Note from *International Standard Bible Encyclopedia*
20. Note from *Strong's Concordance*, #G99

About the Author

James D. Hinson (J.D. as he is known to family and friends) graduated from L.I.F.E. Bible College in 1975 with a Bachelor of Arts Degree in Los Angeles, California.

He is licensed and ordained with the International Church of the Foursquare Gospel. He and his wife, Jan, served as youth pastors in Georgia and Texas and pastored for 32 years including 17 years in Abilene, Texas.

After stepping down from full time pastoral ministry in 2007, J.D. ministers in area churches and conferences across denomination lines.

J.D. and Jan currently reside in Abilene, Texas. They have 3 children and 5 grandchildren.

Contact information for comments, questions or speaking engagements.
(325) 660-9389
lookingup@reagan.com
facebook.com/J.D. Hinson